URBAN
TERRORISM

URBAN TERRORISM

Other Books in the Current Controversies Series:

URBAN TERRORISM

David L. Bender, *Publisher*
Bruno Leone, *Executive Editor*

Scott Barbour, *Managing Editor*
Brenda Stalcup, *Senior Editor*

A.E. Sadler, *Book Editor*
Paul A. Winters, *Book Editor*

CURRENT CONTROVERSIES

Photo credit: AP/Wide World

Library of Congress Cataloging-in-Publication Data

Urban terrorism / A.E. Sadler, book editor, Paul A. Winters, book editor.
     p. cm. — (Current controversies)
    Includes bibliographical references and index.
    ISBN 1-56510-410-2 (pbk. : alk. paper). — ISBN 1-56510-411-0
(lib. bdg. : alk. paper)
    1. Terrorism—United States. 2. Terrorism—United States—Prevention.
    I. Sadler, A.E. II. Winters, Paul A., 1965– . III. Series.
HV6432.U73   1996
363.3'2'0973—dc20   96-11849
                                                            CIP

Contents

Chapter 1: Should Americans Fear Urban Terrorism?

Yes: Americans Should Fear Urban Terrorism

No: Americans Should Not Fear Urban Terrorism

Chapter 2: Which Groups Pose an Urban Terrorist Threat?

Chapter 3: Do the Media Encourage Terrorism?

Yes: The Media Encourage Terrorism

No: The Media Do Not Encourage Terrorism

Chapter 4: Do Antiterrorism Measures Threaten Civil Liberties?

Yes: Antiterrorism Measures Threaten Civil Liberties

No: Antiterrorism Measures Do Not Threaten Civil Liberties

Foreword

By definition, controversies are "discussions of questions in which opposing opinions clash" (Webster's Twentieth Century Dictionary Unabridged). Few would deny that controversies are a pervasive part of the human condition and exist on virtually every level of human enterprise. Controversies transpire between individuals and among groups, within nations and between nations. Controversies supply the grist necessary for progress by providing challenges and challengers to the status quo. They also create atmospheres where strife and warfare can flourish. A world without controversies would be a peaceful world; but it also would be, by and large, static and prosaic.

The Series' Purpose

The purpose of the Current Controversies series is to explore many of the social, political, and economic controversies dominating the national and international scenes today. Titles selected for inclusion in the series are highly focused and specific. For example, from the larger category of criminal justice, Current Controversies deals with specific topics such as police brutality, gun control, white collar crime, and others. The debates in Current Controversies also are presented in a useful, timeless fashion. Articles and book excerpts included in each title are selected if they contribute valuable, long-range ideas to the overall debate. And wherever possible, current information is enhanced with historical documents and other relevant materials. Thus, while individual titles are current in focus, every effort is made to ensure that they will not become quickly outdated. Books in the Current Controversies series will remain important resources for librarians, teachers, and students for many years.

In addition to keeping the titles focused and specific, great care is taken in the editorial format of each book in the series. Book introductions and chapter prefaces are offered to provide background material for readers. Chapters are organized around several key questions that are answered with diverse opinions representing all points on the political spectrum. Materials in each chapter include opinions in which authors clearly disagree as well as alternative opinions in which authors may agree on a broader issue but disagree on the possible solutions. In this way, the content of each volume in Current Controversies mirrors the mosaic of opinions encountered in society. Readers will quickly realize that there are many viable answers to these complex issues. By questioning each author's conclusions, students and casual readers can begin to develop the critical thinking skills so important to evaluating opinionated material.

Current Controversies is also ideal for controlled research. Each anthology in the series is composed of primary sources taken from a wide gamut of informational categories including periodicals, newspapers, books, United States and foreign government documents, and the publications of private and public organizations. Readers will find factual support for reports, debates, and research papers covering all areas of important issues. In addition, an annotated table of contents, an index, a book and periodical bibliography, and a list of organizations to contact are included in each book to expedite further research.

Perhaps more than ever before in history, people are confronted with diverse and contradictory information. During the Persian Gulf War, for example, the public was not only treated to minute-to-minute coverage of the war, it was also inundated with critiques of the coverage and countless analyses of the factors motivating U.S. involvement. Being able to sort through the plethora of opinions accompanying today's major issues, and to draw one's own conclusions, can be a complicated and frustrating struggle. It is the editors' hope that Current Controversies will help readers with this struggle.

"Terrorism results from various causes that defy any clear distinction 'between the political and the criminal.'"

Introduction

The definition of terrorism lies in the gray area that exists between crime and war, although experts disagree as to its approximate location. Some professionals who have spent their careers closely following the various competing theories have resigned themselves to the conclusion that terrorism resists classification. According to professor of international politics Colin S. Gray, terrorism results from various causes that defy any clear distinction "between the political and the criminal."

Some people primarily equate terrorism with war. Noted scholar Noam Chomsky, for one, cites a section of U.S. code that describes terrorism as "the calculated use of violence or threat of violence to attain goals that are political, religious, or ideological." Chomsky argues that this definition of terrorism is essentially the definition of war: It is something that "is conducted by them against us," with "them" meaning an enemy.

Other people describe terrorism as an alternative or substitute for war. Thomas Powers, whose viewpoint is included here, argues that terrorism has served to quench Western nations' propensity for war during the ahistorically long era of peace following World War II. He contends that leftist groups such as Germany's Baader-Meinhof Gang, Italy's Red Brigades, and the United States' less successful Weathermen, by committing a series of bombings, kidnappings, and hijackings, satisfied their nations' need for war. "Looked at this way," Powers writes, "terrorism was a symptom of long fermenting furies—a kind of three day drunk by Western nations, addicted to war and violence." Conversely, Powers maintains, in the Middle East during this same period, terrorism represented the means to avoid completely abandoning existing wars. L. Paul Bremer of Kissinger Associates supports this premise, contending that terrorism made political sense for Middle Eastern nations as "a low-cost, deniable means of continuing their struggle against Israel and its prime supporter, the United States." Terrorism, according to this perspective, was affordable for these North African nations both militarily and politically, whereas outright war was not.

Others believe that terrorism equals crime. They argue that efforts to combat terrorism must be accompanied by efforts to strip away any perception of political legitimacy for the stated motivations behind terrorist acts. Bremer contends that, in the past, "publicity-savvy terrorists have portrayed themselves as modern Robin Hoods who punished the rich on behalf of the downtrodden" and have fooled many Westerners into supporting their causes. "A terrorist who bombs a building commits arson, which is against the law," insists Bremer. "A man who takes a hostage is guilty of kidnapping, which is also against the law. And a politically motivated assassination is murder."

Not everyone agrees with this assessment. Terrorism, to some, is substantially more serious than crime. And by equating crime with terrorism, they argue, experts run the risk of granting criminals a degree of infamy similar to that afforded to terrorists. Journalist Stephen Budiansky regards the October 1995 derailing of an Amtrak passenger train in Arizona, which killed one person and injured more than 100 others, as one such instance. "The eagerness of everyone from the local sheriff to the president of the United States to label the tragedy an act of 'terrorism,'" he complains, "bespeaks a human foible that too many these days share." Such labeling, Budiansky continues, paradoxically rewards "thugs, pranksters and nutcases" for committing offenses by giving them an in-flated sense of importance. To qualify as terrorism, he contends, an act must "threaten to undermine the foundations of American society," which the Amtrak derailment, in his opinion, did not do.

Defining terrorism, as the viewpoints collected in this anthology demonstrate, is no easy matter. *Urban Terrorism: Opposing Viewpoints* explores this issue in addition to other topics, including the tension between counterterrorism efforts and democratic ideals, the factors that contribute to the making of a terrorist, the interaction of the media and terrorism, and the degree to which terrorism poses a threat to people living in the United States.

Chapter 1

Should Americans Fear Urban Terrorism?

Chapter Preface

Nineteen ninety-five was an active year for terrorists in America: On April 19th, the federal building in Oklahoma City was bombed. Among the 167 people killed, 19 were children. On September 19th, a treatise appeared in the *Washington Post* written by a terrorist known as the Unabomber. He had threatened to kill more people if the paper refused to publish his manifesto. The following month, Sheik Omar Abdel Rahman and several of his followers were convicted of plotting to blow up the World Trade Center and several other New York landmarks. Fear reached as far west as Arizona, where someone removed 29 spikes from a train track and caused the derailment of an Amtrak train, an event that occurred within days of the Rahman verdict.

"A line has been crossed," writes *Los Angeles Times* reporter David Wise. "We have become a vulnerable society." Americans, many of whom had previously thought their country immune to terrorism, were stunned by this wave of attacks. Some predict that nuclear terrorism is imminent. Others argue that, as the sole remaining world superpower, the United States now represents the most symbolically important target for terrorists, which simultaneously makes it all the more vulnerable.

While many Americans are horrified by the events of 1995, not everyone agrees that they resulted from, or indicate, a huge breach in security. Some people contend that the shock and dismay with which Americans have reacted reveal not that the nation has grown more vulnerable to terrorism but that it has previously been lucky. Citizens of other countries routinely face terrorist threats, these commentators argue, and people living in the United States are only now beginning to recognize that they, too, may become targets. "Many in the Old World have been looking on with an experienced and somewhat paternalistic eye," writes *New York Times* journalist Serge Schemann, "as if to say, 'Welcome to the club.'" Some believe that the prosperity enjoyed by the United States throughout the latter half of the twentieth century has spoiled its citizens into a naive and unwarranted sense of entitlement regarding their personal safety and well-being. "We seem to think we have a right to security, that it can be bought or voted for," argues Joe Klein. "It can't."

Whether Americans should fear terrorism, both abroad and at home, is the focus of the following chapter. Authors question the degree to which American culture itself may engender the violence of terrorism, as well as the risks posed by nuclear weapons.

America Is Increasingly Vulnerable to Terrorism

by Robin Wright, Ronald J. Ostrow, and Marlene Cimons

About the authors: *Robin Wright, Ronald J. Ostrow, and Marlene Cimons are staff writers for the* Los Angeles Times.

Editor's note: The following viewpoint was published the day after the April 19, 1995, bombing of the Alfred P. Murrah Federal Building in Oklahoma City, Oklahoma.

The World Trade Center. And now Oklahoma City.

Grim reality has been crowding steadily closer.

The age of innocence is ending as Americans realize that terrorism is no longer something threatening other people in other countries.

The End of Innocence

In fact, say federal officials and independent experts, it was an illusion from the beginning. A combination of luck, good intelligence work and efficient law enforcement have prevented scores of attempts at terrorist acts over the last 25 years, according to the Federal Bureau of Investigation (FBI).

"International terrorism" first entered the modern lexicon three decades ago as leftist guerrilla movements clashed with rightist regimes in Latin America. From there, it spread around the world—most notably to the Middle East, where car bombs, like the one that shattered the federal office building in Oklahoma City, are now part of everyday life.

But if America had remained relatively unscathed until the 1993 bombing of the World Trade Center in New York City, any hope of continuing immunity ended once and for all Wednesday, April 19, 1995.

The hulking concrete and steel shreds of the Alfred P. Murrah Federal Building drove the point home even more forcefully than the trade center bombing because of the very ordinariness of the target.

Hitting in America's heartland—instead of a big, urban financial center—

Robin Wright, Ronald J. Ostrow, and Marlene Cimons, "Illusion of Immunity Is Shattered," *Los Angeles Times*, April 20, 1995, p. A1; © 1995 Los Angeles Times. Reprinted with permission.

illustrates the vulnerability of virtually everyone. There is at least one almost identical—and identically vulnerable—federal office center in each of the 50 states.

"This shakes the fundamental faith people have in their security across this country," said Dave McCurdy, a former Oklahoma congressman who served on the House Intelligence Committee.

From day-care centers in Dayton, Ohio, to shopping malls in Seattle, cities and citizens are likely to feel more exposed and more vulnerable. And rightly so, experts say.

"Welcome to the 21st Century. Terrorist attacks in the United States are only going to get worse," said Bruce Hoffman, a former terrorism specialist at the RAND think tank in Santa Monica, California, who now works at St. Andrews University in Scotland.

"The World Trade Center should have been a wake-up call, but it was instead widely seen as the act of amateurs and not a continuing threat. Because it worked in sowing terror, it was certain to happen again. This bombing takes that process one step further."

> *"Terrorist attacks in the United States are only going to get worse."*

To keep the threat in perspective, most experts do not expect that the United States will experience the relentless waves of terrorist attacks that shattered Lebanon and are sweeping over such countries as Algeria.

"We're not on the front lines of a wave of mass terrorism in the United States," said L. Paul Bremer, former head of the State Department's Counterterrorism Office and now a consultant at Kissinger & Associates.

"We're vulnerable, yes, but we have to be realistic. While we can't protect every federal building in this country, from now on we'll all be more careful."

Freedom Makes an Easier Target

What could worsen the social and political impact of terrorism in the United States is the difficulty that both the government and the public will have in taking effective steps to prevent or limit future attacks.

Open borders, the sheer size of the country, the difficulty in monitoring illegal immigrants, the right and necessity of individual access to government facilities and a host of other factors integral to American life hamper the ability to control or seriously limit the threat, experts said.

"We're very good investigators. We will be able to put together the fragments of that bomb and figure out what it was and the method of making it and who has that method. But we'll have a problem in a free country preventing these attacks," said Victoria Toensing, former deputy assistant attorney general for counterterrorism.

"Democracies are by far the most vulnerable to terrorism, because freedoms are used by terrorists to victimize us. Police don't have the right and shouldn't have for sweeps and searches," added Oliver B. Revell, a former top FBI official in charge of anti-terrorism and now a private security consultant.

The difficulties Americans will face were foreshadowed in London during the 1990–91 Persian Gulf crisis. Unprecedented security measures were taken there to thwart terrorist attacks that officials feared might be launched by Iraq, especially against the prime minister's residence and other key government buildings.

Yet despite these measures, a cell of the Irish Republic Army (IRA) managed to get to within a block of the prime minister's historic home and fire a mortar at it as the British Cabinet was meeting. The shell missed the building and landed in the back garden.

At other times, to prevent IRA attacks, side streets throughout London's financial center were closed off and main arteries were tightly monitored by police officers and remote-controlled video cameras.

"Those tactics may have some impact in a country with one major city but you can't hermetically seal off any city from terrorist attacks," Hoffman said. "And that's *really* unrealistic in a country like the United States with dozens of major cities."

Ironically, the Oklahoma City attack comes after major inroads in dealing with terrorism.

In 1994, there was not a single act of terrorism by either domestic or foreign groups in the United States. And international terrorism in 1994 was at a 23-year-low.

In its annual report, the State Department Counterterrorism Office shows that attacks against American targets overseas were more than halved. In 1992, according to the report, 142 incidents were recorded. In 1994, there were 66.

But numbers can be deceiving.

"These statistics are not a reliable index of the threat," Philip C. Wilcox Jr., State Department coordinator for counterterrorism, said in congressional testimony.

"Terrorists have expanded their global reach and today all nations and continents are vulnerable. Moreover, as governments have improved security for their officials and installations, terrorists are striking more frequently at soft, unprotected civilian targets."

And in a hauntingly prescient addendum, Wilcox noted that terrorists are increasingly aiming at mass civilian casualties to increase the fear and disruption that they hope to inflict—

> *"U.S. information, transportation, medical and financial infrastructures are increasingly vulnerable to disruption by terrorists."*

and in the process "far overshadowing" the decline in numbers of non-lethal incidents.

U.S. information, transportation, medical and financial infrastructures are increasingly vulnerable to disruption by terrorists, both foreign and domestic.

Terrorism instigated by cult groups—such as Japan's Aum Supreme Truth, which is suspected of involvement in the March 1995 chemical weapons attack in the Tokyo subway system—is a "pathological phenomenon" even more difficult to anticipate, diagnose and guard against, he said.

The Tokyo attack, and another in Yokohama the following month, also point to the difficulties presented by high-tech and other non-conventional threats including nerve gases and biological weapons.

Almost certainly, the Oklahoma City bombing will provoke calls for tougher anti-terrorism measures.

For one thing, said former FBI official Revell, "the best you can do [now] is use magnetometers and X-ray packages. We've got to do something to give law enforcement the ability at least to collect intelligence on what these groups are doing and saying publicly. The way the law is today, this is something news reporters can do but federal agents cannot."

Learning to Live with It

Yet meaningful steps to bolster the government's anti-terrorism arsenal, including stepped-up efforts by intelligence agencies to monitor individuals and groups inside the United States, are likely to collide with American freedoms.

As the FBI's efforts to discredit Dr. Martin Luther King Jr. and other civil rights leaders during the heyday of former Director J. Edgar Hoover made clear, such powers have a history of turning into abuses.

Perhaps even more serious, the war on terrorism could change the fabric of American life.

"Most of us like to feel that we can protect ourselves in some way or other from danger," said psychologist Dean Kilpatrick, director of the national crime victims research and treatment center in Charleston, South Carolina.

"Even though the fear of crime is something that is very prevalent among Americans, this particular type—no motive, you're minding your own business, in someplace you think should be safe—and all of a sudden, many lives are snuffed out with no way to protect yourself. That's going to have a profound influence on a lot of people."

Others predicted that the death of so many young children in the federal building's day-care center would raise feelings of guilt and fear among working parents, many of whom already struggle with such emotions.

"Working mothers who are generally conflicted about putting their children in day care to pursue careers find this kind of phenomenon exacerbates all those conflicts and guilt feelings," said Rona Fields, an Alexandria, Virginia, psychologist and sociologist.

Yet terrorism specialists also argue that the Oklahoma City bombing is unlikely to be a catalyst for sweeping change.

"What are we going to do? Stop going to work?" said Noel Koch, former Pentagon official in charge of counterterrorism.

"The Europeans have lived with it for years. We'll learn to do it too."

America's Violent Culture Leads to Terrorism

by Adam Gopnik

About the author: *Adam Gopnik is a journalist and contributor to the* New Yorker *magazine.*

"Terror Strikes the Heartland," read one headline, echoing a note widely sounded in the immediate aftermath of the Oklahoma City bombing. But, even before the revelation that this particular atrocity had been as homegrown as a bushel of wheat, the alibi of foreign infection already seemed evasive. For the heartland was in many ways where terror began. The practice of political terrorism has been refined in Europe and the Middle East, but its theory—the understanding that in an age of instant communications killing can be a kind of symbolic speech, a form of show business, engaged in for its publicity value—was pioneered by Americans.

Organic Americanism

It was out West, among the frontier outposts, that the vigilante groups of the mid–nineteenth century—Bald Knobbers, White Caps, and Regulators—developed the practice of killing people in order to send a message. Lynch somebody in New Mexico and they'll get the word in Oregon. Unlike the city-bred (and usually foreign-born) anarchists of a generation or two later, the vigilantes had no interest in notions of universal brotherhood. They saw themselves as personifying an authentic, organic Americanism, the very opposite of the procedural Americanism of laws and legislators and United States marshals. The 1995 bombers in Oklahoma City fit all too well into that bloody tradition, and are all too faithful to its code: Stop thinking of the other person as a person and start thinking of him as an occasion—a blank slate on which to inscribe a Thought for the Day.

The vigilantes were always a weird mixture of fraternal lodge and Murder, Inc., and so are the militias of today. Blood lust shares time with the lure of the secret handshake. The years of the founding of the American West marked the advent of a peculiarly American confusion, from which America has never really emerged: the intertwining of real violence and its romance. Violence gets

Adam Gopnik, "Violence as Style," *New Yorker*, May 8, 1995. Reprinted with permission.

so tangled up with group symbolism that it becomes a demotic idiom, even a kind of slang. Until the moment when the bullet strikes home or the bomb goes off, it all looks disarmingly like Culture. Wild Bill Hickock killed people, and then went on Broadway to show how it was done. Jesse James was a bank robber and a killer, but within seven weeks of his death his wife and his mother had a book ghostwritten explaining that he was just misunderstood—all he was trying to do was make a point on behalf of Confederate war veterans.

Anyone who has spent time reading—"monitoring" is the term of art—the literature of the militias and the survivalists might be forgiven for assuming that they, too, have been engaged in a cultural charade, a game, something like a hobby. For instance, the April 1995 issue of *American Survival Guide*, the consumer magazine of the militia movement, doesn't seem very different in its ingenuous tone and style from an issue of *All Chevy* or *Classic Trucks*, which its publisher, McMullen & Yee, also puts out. An article on raising emus (a kind of ostrich) for fun and profit runs several pages after the column "On Reality," where you can

> *"The understanding that . . . killing can be a kind of symbolic speech, a form of show business, engaged in for its publicity value—was pioneered by Americans."*

read about the Clinton Administration's "abhorrence for the American people" ("They"—the Clinton gang—"must be stopped, if not for us then for our children and for their children"). On one page you can find an ad for a closeout on the 1995 Women & Weaponry Calendar, which features hot-looking babes wearing bandoliers as halter tops, and on the next you can send away for a claymore mine and a bazooka accurate to three hundred yards. In the personals, a lonely guy from Texas announces that he is forming a group "to take action against the up and coming demise of our country," and adds, "The weak hearted need not reply." But another fellow, from Spokane, just wishes to survive "the turmoil of the immature, ignorant and irrational," and is seeking a "survivalist/warrioress/philosopher. The wild nuts tend to turn pretty quickly into pathetic nuts, even likable nuts: in the letters section, a now chilling question asking "Would it be possible for you to advise me as to how I might contact any local militia units in the Midwest?" follows one that hints at the damp reality of Survivalist Weekend Training: "What is the best way to clean/freshen-up a down bag?"

America's Violent Passions

If violence in America leads a kind of double life, as both folk culture and real killing, that double life has produced the peculiarly American overlap of style with action, rhetoric with reality. We are all implicated in this: the intellectual writing for the *Times* who pretends that gangsta rap is part of a continuum with Baptist preaching; the *frisson*-seeking movie critic who wants his "Pulp Fiction" and cannot see that having it might help explain why he cannot allow his children out after five o'clock in the afternoon; and the right-wing thinkers and politicians who have spent fifteen years inventing a demonic abstract enemy called the federal government and now have to explain that they never meant to be taken literally.

Our readiness to explain away violence as style might be called the Anthropological Temptation: everything becomes a hobby, a bit of Americana, a colorful subculture in the pluralistic kaleidoscope. But what happens when the people you patronizingly encouraged, because you thought they were engaged in style and metaphor, turn out to have meant exactly what they said? The American left is familiar with this problem, because it was the left's trendily succumbing to the romance of violence that, more than any other one thing, did it in in the late sixties and early seventies as a serious political force. In those days, the idea that violence was redemptive in itself led Norman Mailer to praise two kids for killing a candy-store owner, and led New Leftists like Peter Collier and David Horowitz (then the editors of *Ramparts*) to become infatuated with the thuggery of the Black Panthers. It wasn't that the left loved violence, exactly, but that the left—or, anyway, too much of it—liked the thrill of seeing its musty intellectual beliefs acted out as dashing cultural theatre. (The left's bombs, though, were often duds, unlike the right's—the difference between the kids who paid attention in social studies and the ones who paid attention in shop.)

"Verbal Napalm"

In the first couple of days after the Oklahoma City horror, conservative commentators clamored to make clear that they, at least, were able to see that you can't separate inflammatory rhetoric from violent acts—that ideas have consequences. Just after the bombing, when it seemed likely that Islamic militants had done it, Rupert Murdoch's New York flagship, the *Post*, was prepared to throw the book not only at the presumed terrorists but at their whole network of ideological support and encouragement—what the *Post* called, scarily, their "terror links." One headline read, "TERROR-LINK GROUPS MET REGULARLY IN OKLAHOMA CITY," and the story described militant Muslim groups as meeting for "jihad conventions," in which various sheikhs say things like "Attend shooting practice. There is nothing greater than the shot." Of course, the right quickly found itself obliged to pull a one-eighty, leaving skid marks and the smell of burning rubber all over the information highway. By Sunday morning—four days after the explosion—George Will and Robert Novak were making delicate civil-libertarian noises about guilt by association and how climates of opinion shouldn't be construed as chains of causal connection. Will followed up with a column on the subject for the Washington *Post*, conceding that ideas produce actions but dismissing the past two years as a cool technocratic debate about "the duties and capacities of government." At the same time, in a *Newsweek* column, evidently written before the Oklahoma City revelations, Will fêted the right-wing congressional fruitcake Robert Dornan (who routinely calls anyone to the left of Bob Dole a traitor), chortling at Dornan's flair for "verbal napalm" and promising that his presence in the Presidential race would make the Republican campaign "more fun than a food fight." Some fun. And by the fifth day, Rush Limbaugh himself was mocking the phrase "right-wing extremists" and rounding up the usual suspects: the fault, he explained, lay with the liberals, who, back in the sixties and seventies, had tied the hands of the Federal Bureau of Investigation (FBI). A couple of months earlier, discussing supposed environmental tramplings on property rights, he predicted, "The second violent American revolution is just about—I got my fingers about a quarter of an inch apart—is just about that far away. Because these people are sick and tired of a bunch of bureaucrats in Washington driving into town and telling them what they can and can't do with their land."

> *"It is no great exaggeration to say that* **American Survival Guide** *is just* **The American Spectator** *with bazooka ads."*

The point, of course, isn't that Limbaugh or Pat Robertson or G. Gordon Liddy caused the killing. It is that they seemed never to have given a moment's thought, as they addressed their audiences, to the consequences of stuffing so much flammable resentment into such tiny bottles. Conservatives are generally clearheaded about the connection between rhetoric and action when it comes to people who are not conservatives. A generation ago, conservatives had no trouble associating "revolutionary" sloganeering of the "by any means necessary" variety with the bomb that shattered the math building at the University of Wisconsin. And when it comes to Leonard Jeffries or Louis Farrakhan today, it is not hard for George Will or Murdoch's *Post* to insist, against the grain of liberal indulgence, that if you daily inject hatred into the bloodstream someone might get sick.

Ideas and Guns

That's a fair point. Timothy McVeigh [the main suspect in the Oklahoma bombing] may be a nut, but nuts don't fall far from the tree. Fifty years from now, historians are unlikely to write, "In the mid-nineties, politicians and talk-show radio hosts created an atmosphere of poisonous hatred against the national government. Also, in a completely unrelated development, somebody blew up the federal office building in Oklahoma City." What they will write is more apt to be something like "In the mid-nineties, an atmosphere of poisonous hatred of the national government was allowed to grow in America; a few right-wing extremists even went as far as to bomb a federal building." The problem is not that the militias have been mysteriously infiltrated by extremists but that the federal government has, especially in the past two years, been inflated into an imaginary hate-object big enough for a nut. That's happened with the enthusiastic help of "mainstream" right-wing paranoia: Bill Clinton is an illegitimate President; liberals are the enemies of normal Americans; gun control is a conspiracy to tyrannize the populace; a New World Order is being put in place by foreign bankers. These are the ideas of Pat Robertson and Pat Buchanan and the National Rifle Association (NRA)—ideas, in other words, that a section of the "responsible" right in this country has spent the last few years legitimating and circulating. It is no great exaggeration to say that *American Survival Guide* is just *The American Spectator* [a conservative monthly magazine] with bazooka ads.

Of course, the difference is that the militia right comes armed with ideas and guns, whereas the mainstream far right comes armed only with ideas. Not a meaningless difference but not a decisive one, either, as we discover when the ideas being promoted are the kind whose logical consequence is to make somebody else want to go pick up a gun. It turns out that there isn't one world of cultural theatre and another world of real acts. The terrorists, though, had come to believe they weren't bombing a building full of people but obliterating an abstract object of hate. The "grievances" that are said to have moved them seem, on examination, curiously bloodless—things seen on television and in "instructional" videos rather than actually experienced. The people who had helped teach them to view the world as a set of easy abstractions, rather than as intricate arrangements made by human beings and inhabited by them, are under no obligation to take the blame for what happened. But it would be nice to see a little remorse.

Nuclear Arms Increase the Threat of Terrorism

by Sharon Begley

About the author: *Sharon Begley is a science reporter for* Newsweek *magazine.*

To bomb New York's World Trade Center in February 1993, the terrorists needed about 1,200 pounds of fuel oil and fertilizer. The mix was sufficient to kill six people and turn three levels of parking garage into a tangle of steel beams. To detonate an explosion in London's financial district two months later, the Irish Republican Army (IRA) used a ton of fertilizer spiked with Semtex explosive. That blast killed one person and blew holes in a dozen buildings. With 1,750 pounds of diesel oil and fertilizer, eight men arrested in New York in June of 1993 figured they could destroy the Lincoln Tunnel and the United Nations.

A Real Nightmare

But as witches' brews go, this is all pretty thin gruel. The true security nightmare is a nuclear weapon locked in a trunk in the parking lot at Washington's Union Station. Even a crude atomic bomb could level buildings for miles around ground zero. The resulting fireball would radiate at the speed of sound, incinerating every bit of steel, concrete and human flesh in its path and igniting a holocaust that would make Dresden look like a birthday candle.

The Biggest Barrier

What's keeping a terrorist group from going nuclear? Building an atomic bomb requires two things: knowledge and material. Knowledge has not been in short supply since the Manhattan Project tests at Alamogordo, New Mexico. A terrorist might start with the $23 hardback "The Los Alamos Primer." On page 25 are the once top-secret data on the minimum amount of uranium needed to sustain a chain reaction. Page 44 explains how to build a reflector to halve the amount of fissionable material required. Page 57 details how to shoot a slug of uranium into a bomb's core and trigger the nuclear explosion. And if the terrorist had a sense of irony, he might check out the 1986 book "Preventing Nuclear

Terrorism": it contains the exact weights of uranium or plutonium needed for a bomb.

The biggest barrier to nuclear terrorism has been material. A bomb needs plutonium or enriched uranium—products too expensive to produce and, until recently, very difficult to steal. With the disintegration of the Soviet Union, however, thousands of nuclear-weapons workers are out of jobs and out of money. But not out of ideas. In 1992 two Russians and a Belarusian swiped 5.5 pounds of semi-enriched uranium pellets from a top-secret plant somewhere in Russia, stuffed them into a lead container and drove 1,200 miles to Brest, Belarus. (Police arrested them before they could strike a deal with their Polish buyers.) German investigators uncovered more than 100 nuclear-smuggling schemes in 1992, compared with 35 in 1991. "What you're talking about with smuggling is the guys guarding the back fence [of an ex-Soviet nuclear facility] and making $10 a month," says David Kay, who headed the United Nations nuclear-inspection team in Iraq after the gulf war. "As you disassemble weapons, of course you should worry."

> *"The true security nightmare is a nuclear weapon locked in a trunk in the parking lot at Washington's Union Station."*

None of the uranium smuggled out of the ex-Soviet states so far has been weapons grade (a purified form of the element, called uranium-235, that sustains a chain reaction). The one known attempt to slip a small quantity of bomb-grade uranium out of Russia was foiled. But what troubles Kay and others is that smuggling routes are being established. "The customs people don't have a clue if their intercepts are the whole universe or much less," says Kay, now at the Uranium Institute in London. The most worrisome routes are not the well-monitored ones to the West but those through Kazakhstan or Georgia to Iraq, Iran, Afghanistan, India and Pakistan. U.S. officials say they have credible evidence that Iranian front companies have tried to acquire nuclear materials from Kazakhstan.

A Cruder Task

Terrorists don't have to produce anything like the complex and efficient bombs in the U.S. and Russian arsenals. Their task would be cruder: create a critical mass in order to make the nucleus of the plutonium or uranium atoms fission and release enormous energy. Either of two simple bomb designs could reprise Hiroshima:

• In a gun-type bomb, a slug of uranium shot from a modified gun barrel boosts a chunk of uranium to critical mass. "If you use weapons-grade uranium, you would need about 50 kilograms [114 pounds]—a little bigger than a soccer ball," says David Albright of the Institute for Science and International Security, a think tank in Washington. That assumes the bomb is surrounded by a reflector, a shell of iron or graphite a few inches thick that bounces neutrons back to the core to sustain the chain reaction. Ordinary machine tools could turn uranium into the requisite sphere; working the metal poses little risk of radiation exposure or explosion. A timer, available at any electronics store, could be wired to the device to shoot the projectile at the desired hour. A gun-type bomb could produce a 15-kiloton blast the size of the Hiroshima bomb. Even if the reaction fizzled short of a mushroom cloud, the shower of radiation from a small blast could kill a few thousand people.

• In an implosion bomb, specially shaped charges studding a sphere of uranium squash it into a critical mass. An "initiator" encased in the fuel provides an extra boost to the chain reaction; a few grains of the element polonium, available in many university physics labs, and lithium, for sale at chemical-supply houses, would work. About 20 pounds of plutonium-239 (or half that with a reflector) would sustain a chain reaction, producing a one-kiloton explosion that could topple skyscrapers. That 20 pounds might not even be missed: the chief engineer of a Russian plant that reprocesses spent uranium into plutonium says, because of bookkeeping uncertainties, 33 pounds of plutonium could vanish every three months without anyone knowing it. "And even if terrorists just have high explosives packed around five to seven kilograms of plutonium," says Albright, "the radioactivity would be terrifying."

Counting Barrels

A team might need no more than a year to master bomb design and obtain uranium. Then it could assemble a workable nuclear bomb "in a few days," says David Fischer of the International Atomic Energy Agency in Vienna. But he calls that scenario "extremely unlikely. Metallurgist terrorists and physicist terrorists are not easy to come by." Maybe so, but no one is doing much to choke off the potential supply. "Nuclear-engineering departments at many American universities are being kept alive by foreign students, including Iraqis, Iranians and Libyans," says Paul Leventhal of the Nuclear Control Institute in Washington. "There's the concept of academic freedom, but there's also the question of who we're educating and why."

Under disarmament treaties, the ex–Soviet Union will dismantle 2,000 nuclear warheads a year until well into the twenty-first century; that will mean moving six tons of plutonium and 30 tons of uranium from easily counted missiles to hard-to-inventory stockpiles. Can anyone monitor it all? While the United States measured uranium stockpiles down to the microgram, the Soviets—claiming a lack of sophisticated measuring devices—counted *barrels* of bomb-grade uranium and pits (softball-size units) of plutonium. Given

> *"Even if terrorists just have . . . five to seven kilograms of plutonium . . . the radioactivity would be terrifying."*

that imprecision, says Kay, "skimming is relatively easy when you're disassembling weapons. Anyone who tells you no material is missing either doesn't know what he's talking about or is deluding himself."

The world is not yet awash in the fuel for bombs. But the spigot has been turned.

America's Vulnerability to Terrorism Is Declining

by Ken Adelman

About the author: *Ken Adelman is a nationally syndicated columnist.*

"Guilty!" the jury forewoman distinctly enunciated 38 times one Friday in early March 1994. Thus ended the trial of the four men accused of the 1993 World Trade Center bombing, which caused six deaths, hundreds of millions of dollars in damage, and our fright of a tough terrorist wave hitting America.

But this does not end Americans' fear of terrorism erupting here, as it has erupted in Western Europe and most brutally in the Middle East and Latin America.

Rather, the verdict reinforces the now-accepted truth that "international terrorism has in fact reached the shores of the United States," as the head of the Federal Bureau of Investigation (FBI) office in New York, William Gavin, said after the verdict was announced.

But is this right? Will terrorism become yet another form of violence inflicting our lives?

It sure seems so. Experts sure say it's so. Still, I doubt it is so.

More Fear than Harm

Terrorism will frighten more than damage us. While individual acts can do major damage, the chances of a terrorist wave hitting here, as it has elsewhere, remain slight.

Granted, facts now point otherwise. That trial concerned the worst terrorist attack ever to hit America. Police had surrounded the Manhattan courthouse, not only because of this verdict but also because of the Hebron massacre and shooting of Hasidic students on the Brooklyn bridge three days prior to the announcement of the verdict.

September 1994 brought another sensational terrorist trial. A dozen followers of Sheik Omar Abdel Rahman, the blind Muslim cleric, were tried for conspiracy to blow up the United Nations, the Holland and Lincoln tunnels, and other central spots in New York.

In 1993, four other men were indicted in Washington for planning to blow up the Israeli Embassy.

Ken Adelman, "Incoming Tide of Terrorism?" *Washington Times*, March 9, 1994. Reprinted by permission: Tribune Media Services.

Besides these facts, logic also points to terrorism on the rise. As Israel's biggest backer and the world's prime secular democratic state, the United States should be Muslim fanatics' No. 1 target.

And as the world's most open society, the United States should be the easiest target. Our cities are most vulnerable. After all, New York City barely squeaks by under the most ideal conditions.

So why my doubting of the conventional wisdom?

Because: (1) the international terrorist network has dried up; (2) terrorism has proven politically unproductive; and (3) anti-terrorism technology and intelligence-gathering are improving fast. Yes, Virginia, there was an international terrorist network. What was long doubted, especially during the Reagan years, has since been substantiated. In May 1992, Boris Yeltsin released a stack of documents on the Soviets' organizing and funding a worldwide terrorist network.

The KGB spent at least $20 million a year, a hefty sum for a fanatical band which operated cheaply and needed only small arms and primitive bombs. The World Trade Center bomb, for instance, cost only $400.

The KGB's sister organizations helped, too. East Germans specialized as spies and dirty tricksters. Czechs furnished small arms and bombs. Bulgarian agents apparently swung deadly umbrellas and may have assisted the 1981 assassination attempt against the pope. Other Warsaw Pact members hosted terrorist training camps and helped in sundry other ways.

"Terrorism will frighten more than damage us."

All this is gone now. The absence of a supporting network was first evident in 1990, when Saddam Hussein called for a wave of anti-Western terrorism after Desert Shield began, and no one came.

Second, terrorism has proven a political bust. It can damage in specific ways—nearly killing Egypt's tourism industry, for example—but does nothing to advance a political cause.

Libya's Moammar Gadhafi, the Irish Republican Army, the Red Brigade and other vile types learned that holding hostages or blowing up buildings arouses, not sympathy and accommodation, but fury and resistance. Responsible Islamic leaders in America must now overcome the stain of these trials, which do nothing but damage to the Palestinians' cause.

Outwitting Terrorism

Third, the technological and intelligence balance has shifted from terrorists to law-enforcers. The 1995 trial of the "dirty dozen" for conspiring to bomb seemingly dozens of prime New York sites promised to be sensational.

But, still, this is a trial about a massive conspiracy of terrorist attacks that did not happen.

Experience with terrorism in Europe, the Middle East and Latin America has spurred a whole new industry of better detection and anti-terrorism technology. Moreover, the Cold War's end has freed up agents to become human detectors.

Employing Parkinson's most astute law—that the success of any policy is measured by the catastrophes that do not ensue—our anti-terrorism policy has generally been a roaring success. Despite the worry today, I expect it to stay such.

American Violence Does Not Contribute to Domestic Terrorism

by Thomas Powers

About the author: *Contributing editor to the* Los Angeles Times *newspaper, Thomas Powers won a Pulitzer prize for his coverage of the 1970 Weatherman bombing incident. He recently published* Heisenberg's War: The Secret History of the German Bomb.

Americans worried that terrorism is about to join the catalog of national ills ought to reflect on March 6, 1970, a date that means nothing to most of them. In New York City on that day, in the basement of a townhouse on a pleasant, tree-lined street in the neighborhood known as Greenwich Village, two men and a woman in their 20s took the first step in what they hoped would be a campaign of relentless and merciless urban terrorism.

Repeated attacks, they hoped, would spark a law-and-order backlash leading, in turn, to revolution, violent overthrow of the government in Washington and imposition of a communist dictatorship that would end capitalism and root out all trace of liberal bourgeois faith in private property, the Bill of Rights and democracy by majority rule.

That was the plan, anyhow.

The Wrong Wire

What the aspirant terrorists actually did that morning was to assemble a bundle of dynamite sticks, wrap them in duct tape studded with galvanized roofing nails and attach a detonator wired to a cheap alarm clock. At the appointed hour the bomb would announce that terrorism had arrived in the United States. First to know would be the ruling elite of corporate America in their three-piece suits as they hurried through Grand Central Station to catch the 5:10 p.m. to Connecticut.

One can easily imagine what a bomb would do in such a crowd. If all had gone according to plan, the date would be fixed in the national memory. But fate, luck, divine Providence, plain ignorance of things technical—in short, the wrong wire—intervened. The bomb killed the young woman assembling it with such violence she had to be identified by the tip of a little finger. Her two companions died as well. The rest of the group, known as the Weatherman faction of the Students for a Democratic Society, disappeared into hiding and their plan for terrorism leading to revolution ended on its first day.

"Gun violence is as American as cherry pie. It is clandestine political violence which has never taken root in the United States."

But elsewhere in the world at the same time, events unfolded far differently: In Northern Ireland, the Irish Republican Army had already begun a campaign to drive the British out of the six counties; Germany lived in fear of a left-wing group of young kidnappers and assassins known as the Baader-Meinhof Gang; Italian radicals were organizing the Red Brigades; the Red Army Faction in Japan would soon be killing members who failed tests of ideological purity, and in the Middle East, Palestinian extremists, in a host of small underground groups, had begun a program of aircraft hijackings and attacks on innocent civilians.

Terrorist groups tend to be self-absorbed, making it all the more difficult to explain the global phenomenon of like-minded, mostly young, mostly middle-class, mostly Marxist-Leninist killers that emerged in the late '60s and early '70s. Also common to the first groups was a quixotic impracticality—their means were hopelessly unequal to their goals—and a tendency, encouraged by failure, to turn their ferocity upon themselves.

The Weathermen endured a miserable few years of underground fear and recrimination before they resurfaced, one by one, to pay a modest debt to society for old crimes and then take up professional roles. The exception was Kathy Boudin, who escaped the townhouse bombing but was arrested in 1981, following a failed raid on an armored car in Nyack, New York, and is now serving a long prison sentence.

A Gothic Horror

But elsewhere, the fate of spiritual brothers and sisters reached a level of gothic horror. In Germany, Andreas Baader, Ulrike Meinhof and other leaders all committed suicide in jail, several with smuggled guns on the same day in an attempt to make it appear as if they had been murdered by police. In Japan, a Red Army group spent a long winter in a cabin on the slopes of Mt. Fuji, arguing politics. From time to time, one of the members, failing to follow the political line argued by the others closely enough, would be stripped naked, bound with wire and thrown out into the snow to freeze to death. The ethos of violence in all terrorist groups is a threat first to themselves, but among the Irish and the Palestinians, factional murders, though frequent, have never taken precedence over the war against their enemies—the British and the Israelis, respectively.

Some observers have speculated that the worldwide pandemic of terrorism is only a kind of substitute for war. A combination of nuclear weapons and the global net of Soviet and U.S. alliances in the Cold War, the argument goes, made war too dangerous, and conflicts were routinely nipped in the bud.

In Western Europe, especially, a kind of unnatural peace reigned long beyond the customary generation that separates big wars. Looked at in this way, terrorism was a symptom of long-fermenting furies—a kind of three-day drunk by Western nations, addicted to war and violence, following too long a stretch of unnaturally good behavior. In the Middle East, unmistakably, terrorism was a continuation of war by other means.

But no country has been less often invaded or longer at peace than the United States, where most citizens have never shouldered arms or even seen an army in the field. The national and ethnic tensions of Europe and the Middle East are fully matched by American racial animosities but the latter have never generated the same level of clandestine violence with a political purpose.

Violence, American-Style

But of violence itself there is plenty. Few countries, and none called modern, can match the sheer level of violence in the United States, where 24,000 homicides are recorded annually, and the street battles of drug gangs make Dodge City in its heyday sound like Arcadia.

The St. Valentine's Day Massacre in Chicago during bootlegging days, when the execution of seven men shocked the world, is now repeated almost weekly in America's inner cities, and the victims, as often as not, include women or children who happen to be present. Some of this violence has been imported from Latin countries, where men of power routinely travel in armored cars and employ body guards with submachine guns. But gun violence is as American as cherry pie.

> *"Americans ought to remember March 6, 1970, when a misplaced wire ended three young lives and a campaign of terrorism before it began."*

It is clandestine political violence which has never taken root in the United States. Puerto Rican nationalists perhaps came closest in the 1940s and '50s, with an unsuccessful attack on President Harry S. Truman and a brief burst of machine-gun fire in the U.S. Congress. Much more typical were the efforts of the Weathermen, and yet more isolated acts of terror—a bomb detonated in a crowd of police in Chicago in 1886, a devastating blast on Wall Street in 1929, which killed innocent passersby when a bomb went off without warning or later explanation.

These outrages, lethal as they were, probably made less of an impression on the nation's consciousness than the series of mostly harmless bombs set throughout New York in the 1950s by George Metesky, known as the Mad Bomber. His purpose, confessed after he was caught, was to protest callous treatment by Consolidated Edison 20 years earlier.

Attention but Not Results

The World Trade Center bombing in New York, on February 26, 1993, killing six, has prompted a round of fears that terrorism was about to plunge the

United States into a violent nightmare. Similar fears swept the country twice before—during the Gulf War in early 1991, when authorities worried that Iraq's Saddam Hussein would blow up nuclear reactors and poison city water supplies; and in 1983, when Americans simply crossed Europe off their vacation lists for fear of Islamic terrorists seeking vengeance for the accidental downing of an Iranian passenger plane by a U.S. warship.

Now, as then, prudent caution requires the authorities to treat all threats seriously. But Americans ought to remember March 6, 1970, when a misplaced wire ended three young lives and a campaign of terrorism before it began. Terror never wins wars, but only keeps causes alive by what anarchists used to call "the propaganda of the deed."

The prosaic truth is that the United States offers an alternative to the hardships of life underground in political war against the system: polls, press agents and political-action committees get results where bombs only get attention. It was anger, not conviction they knew how to change the world, that brought the Weathermen to their basement bomb factory in Greenwich Village, and though survivors have been too proud to confess the fact, it was anger that died there.

The Threat of Nuclear Terrorism Is Minimal

by Brian M. Jenkins

About the author: *Brian M. Jenkins serves as deputy chairman to Kroll Associates, an international investigative firm.*

Nineteen ninety-five began with renewed alarms about terrorism. Car bombs exploded in Algiers, Algeria, and in Beit Lid, Israel. One of the key suspects in the 1993 bombing of the World Trade Center was arrested in Pakistan and extradited to the United States. Fearing that his comrades, still at large, might retaliate by planting bombs aboard airliners, authorities heightened airport security worldwide. Airlines flying in Europe and North Africa were already on edge following the December 1994 hijacking of an Air France jet by Algerian extremists, who, according to French authorities, intended to blow up the plane over Paris. Chechen rebels threatened to launch a campaign of terrorism in Russia. The discovery of a cache of explosives in Buenos Aires renewed fears of further large-scale terrorist bombings similar to those that occurred in 1992 and 1994. In March, a poison gas attack on the Tokyo subway marked a startling and ominous development.

Will Terrorists Go Nuclear?

President Clinton used his State of the Union address to call for "renewed fervor in a global effort to combat terrorism." Ironically, that effort would begin at home. On April 19 of the same year, a truck loaded with nearly 5,000 pounds of homemade explosives blew up in front of the federal building in Oklahoma City, killing 168. It was the worst terrorist bombing in U.S. history. Clearly, it is necessary to rethink terrorism. Will terrorism persist? Have terrorists crossed a threshold into the domain of mass murder? Will they hold cities hostage? Will terrorists go nuclear? Or will we simply see more of the same? Although it is perilous to predict what small groups of extremists might do in the future, it is possible to paint a picture of the future in broad brush strokes. . . .

The fall of the Soviet Union has eliminated a source of ideological inspiration and operational assistance for terrorism. Soviet support for national liberation movements, which the Gorbachev regime had already reduced, has ended. Ter-

Excerpted from Brian M. Jenkins, "The Limits of Terror: Constraints on the Escalation of Violence," *Harvard International Review*, vol. 17, no. 3 (Summer 1995). Reprinted by permission.

rorists from the Middle East can no longer depend on safe passage, and terrorists from Western Europe can no longer find refuge in Eastern Europe. Having lost Soviet support, the political maneuvering capability of those Middle Eastern and North African states accused of sponsoring terrorism has been reduced. Deprived of Soviet help, they have been forced to look West.

The collapse of communism has also dampened the psychological impact of terrorism. Measured against the destructive capability of war, terrorist actions were always a minor threat. The fear of terrorism, however, reflected deeper anxieties about nuclear war—hence our fascination with the possibility of nuclear terrorism. Dramatic acts of violence provided real life villains who personified shapeless fears. The collapse of the Soviet Union and the military victory of the United States over Iraq helped to reduce these worries.

Victories of Violence

Not all recent developments have been favorable. Although the threat of global nuclear war has diminished, the threat of nuclear proliferation has increased. While the fall of the Soviet Union has eliminated ideology as a principal engine of conflict, ethnic or tribal hostility and religious extremism continue to drive numerous medium and small wars and inspire enormous atrocities. And, if the collapse of communism has discouraged some terrorists, other events may be seen as vindications of terrorism. Through their tactics, terrorists have gained media attention and occasional concessions, caused alarm, diverted vast resources to security agencies, provoked repression, and slowed the resolution of conflicts. Terrorists, however, have historically not been able to convert these tactical successes into concrete political gains. There are now two potential exceptions. Palestinian terrorism kept its cause alive, even after Arab armies had been defeated on the field. Spectacular acts of violence undoubtedly contributed to a sense of Palestinian nationhood, obliged—sometimes through threats—Arab governments to finance the movement, and ultimately forced the Israelis to treat it as a legitimate political entity. Although it would be erroneous to view the recent Palestinian gains, which many Palestinians consider a sellout, as a terrorist triumph, terrorism did play a significant role.

> *"Using the weapons they have had for decades, terrorists could have killed in greater quantities had that been their sole objective. Not doing so represents a choice."*

On another front, the United Kingdom has taken the first steps toward a political settlement which, at least tacitly, recognizes the Irish Republican Army (IRA). One could legitimately doubt that the British government would have agreed to negotiations had there been no continual campaign of terrorism in Northern Ireland, no persistent drain on the national budget from security expenditures, and no horrifying threat of never-ending terrorist violence in England. Bombs and guns undeniably encouraged political creativity. Desperate men, as all terrorists are, will view these cases as victories of violence. Terrorism will thus remain a threat for the foreseeable future. What will it look like?

Chapter 1

The Terrorist Map

Without entering the realm of prophesy, we have no way of forecasting what incidents of terrorism might soon occur. We can, however, offer some observations about longer-term trends in terrorism. With more than a quarter century of closely analyzed terrorist incidents to draw upon, we can identify trends in terrorist tactics, weapons, and targets. Although terrorist attacks intrude upon our consciousness in brief violent episodes, terrorism, as a phenomenon, evolves more slowly. A significant portion of all terrorist attacks are the product of armed conflicts that have continued for decades. The map of terrorist activity tomorrow will closely resemble that of today.

Past experience has taught us a good deal about how terrorists plan their actions. For reasons we will come to, terrorists generally appear to be conservative planners, more imitative than innovative and reluctant to depart from well-worn paths. Terrorism's trajectory is thus, to a degree, predictable, although each terrorist attack comes as a surprise. Still, there are contentious issues within the tiny community of analysts of terrorism, such as whether or not terrorists will attack society's technological frailties in order to cause widespread disruption, go nuclear, or employ other weapons of mass destruction in order to cause widespread casualties. Experts disagree.

> *"There is ... no evidence that any terrorist group has sought to acquire nuclear material or even ... seriously contemplated going nuclear."*

Some foresee the emergence of "super-terrorists." These high-tech villains will use weaponry far more sophisticated than that in today's terrorist arsenal; hold cities hostage with a stolen or clandestinely fabricated chemical, biological, or nuclear weapon; or cause widespread disruption by attacking vital systems such as the waterworks, the food chain, public transportation, or the energy grid. Some foresee the emergence of "white collar terrorists" who will focus their attacks on information and communication systems, the nervous system of modern society. On the other side of the debate are those who argue that tomorrow's terrorist is likely to be a somewhat more violent clone of today's terrorist—high on dedication, but often barely competent, exhibiting little innovation in tactics, weapons, or targets, except for a drift toward indiscriminate violence. The debate, of course, is entirely theoretical. There is much to suggest, however, that terrorists will stick to well-worn paths.

The form of terrorist violence has changed little in the past 30 years. Terrorists continue to operate with the limited tactical repertoire they developed in the late 1960s and early 1970s. Bombings account for about half of all terrorist attacks. The remaining incidents consist of political murders, hostage-takings, drive-by shootings, and stand-off attacks. Terrorists appear to be conservative planners. Success is vital; failure erodes morale and loses members. Consensus must be maintained, and uncertainty threatens consensus in addition to risking failure. Consequently, terrorist groups possess a low tolerance for innovation. Moreover, terrorists can solve most tactical problems merely by switching targets, and since targets for terrorists are virtually unlimited, the need for tactical innovation is further reduced.

"Hobby-Shop" Technology

If tactics remain the same, there is little need to alter weapons. The weapons commonly used by terrorists—handguns, submachine guns, and rocket-propelled grenades—represent Second World War technology. Their explosives range from primitive pipe bombs to sophisticated devices. This has been their area of greatest technological innovation. Terrorists have employed "hobby-shop" technology to launch radio-controlled cars and model boats carrying explosives. They have also used mortars and rocket launchers. Some are even believed to possess hand-held surface-to-air missiles, but only guerrilla groups operating in rural areas have used them. Possibly because they lack the opportunity to practice with the weapons or because they fear an uncontrollable escalation, urban-based terrorist groups have not yet used these missiles. On the other hand, perhaps they are simply waiting for the appropriate moment or target.

Beginning in the 1980s, there has been a growing trend toward indiscriminate attacks as terrorists have planted bombs in public places. Car bombings, for example, have evidently increased in frequency, with more than 100 between 1993 and 1995. Its destructive potential notwithstanding, the car bomb's principal feature is quantity, not quality—it is not a high-tech weapon. Indiscriminate violence, however, does not equal mass murder. Even most car bombs, although parked in public areas, are detonated at night or with a warning in order to reduce casualties. The average number of fatalities per car bombing is 20, while the median is five.

Outside of war, deliberate attempts to kill as many people as possible in one violent action are rare. We find few precedents in the annals of contemporary terrorism. Terrorists want many witnesses, not many dead. Terrorists employ violence to achieve ends other than murder for murder's sake. Using the weapons they have had for decades, terrorists could have killed in greater quantities had that been their sole objective. Not doing so represents a choice, not a technical limitation.

Terrorists are governed by self-imposed constraints, including their own moral qualms and their concerns about cohesion. Even those organizations that we label terrorist view themselves as political or military organizations, not as wanton killers. A group using terrorist tactics must take care not to push members, who may not have the stomach for certain acts of violence, toward defection. Terrorists also worry about alienating their perceived supporters, whom they imagine to be a legion even if less committed than themselves. While terrorists want to provoke fear and alarm, they do not want to provoke too great a public backlash. Fear of unleashing government crackdowns that have popular support is another brake on terrorist violence. . . .

> *"I . . . see terrorists in terms of motives—a mixture of ideologues, fanatics, adventurers, and thugs, who are . . . fascinated with violence but constrained in its application."*

Chapter 1

The Black Market

Recent reports of plutonium and highly enriched uranium being smuggled out of Russia have raised concerns about the emergence of a nuclear black market and the specter of nuclear terrorism. Recent arrests reveal that there are sellers who have access to at least small quantities of fissile materials. Potential buyers, other than undercover policemen conducting sting operations, exist in theory; but none have actually been identified, although authorities in Japan found in the notes belonging to one of the leaders of the sect responsible for the Tokyo subway attack a reference to the possibility of purchasing a nuclear weapon in Russia. That does not mean that such a trade could not develop in the future. There is, however, no evidence that any terrorist group has sought to acquire nuclear material or even that terrorists have seriously contemplated going nuclear.

Although the words "nuclear" and "terrorism" in close proximity undoubtedly would provoke great alarm, it is doubtful that terrorists could translate a nuclear threat into commensurate coercive power. There are limits to extortion. Not only would terrorists have to convince authorities that they had nuclear capability, but they would also have to persuade them that compliance with their demands would end the threat. Without credibility on both counts, there would be little incentive for authorities to comply. It may be easier to employ a nuclear device as an instrument of destruction than as an instrument of coercion. Had the bombers of the World Trade Center somehow acquired a nuclear device, they probably would have used it.

As fissile material and the secrets of nuclear weapons design become widely available, nuclear capabilities may reach groups willing to use them. Many strategic analysts, in fact, consider a nuclear terrorism scenario more likely than a nuclear war. It would, however, be a giant step in terrorist technology and tactics. Lesser acts of nuclear terrorism such as the use of radioactive material as a contaminant or the fabrication of potentially alarming nuclear hoaxes may be more plausible. . . .

Robert Kupperman, as a scientist, sees terrorists in terms of capabilities that could be acquired and that would enable terrorists to ascend to higher levels of sophistication and violence. I have tended to see terrorists in terms of motives—a mixture of ideologues, fanatics, adventurers, and thugs, who are action-prone, fascinated with violence but constrained in its application. Sometimes they are technically sophisticated; often they are barely competent.

Kupperman, a theorist, warns of future dangers. As more of an empiricist, I point to past behavior and despite recent developments see no inexorable progress toward mass destruction. Admittedly, this approach may be too rationalist in two senses. First, it rests upon the presumption that an objective analysis of history will yield some indications of its future course. Second, it may presume rational behavior on the part of desperate men of sometimes dionysian passions. Only future events will provide the definitive answer.

Chapter 2

Which Groups Pose an Urban Terrorist Threat?

CURRENT CONTROVERSIES

Chapter Preface

A little after 9:00 a.m. on April 19, 1995, a bomb made from a mixture of fertilizer and fuel oil destroyed the Alfred P. Murrah Federal Building in Oklahoma City, killing 167 people. Within days, agents of the Federal Bureau of Investigation (FBI) arrested Timothy McVeigh and Terry Nichols as suspects in the bombing, but law enforcement officials could only theorize about the two men's motives. One possible motive was suggested by Morris Dees of the Southern Poverty Law Center (SPLC), which monitors the activities of right-wing and racist groups. The day after the bombing, Dees speculated that it was an act of retaliation for the FBI's 1993 raid on the Branch Davidian compound in Waco, Texas. The raid—a fifty-one-day standoff ending on April 19, 1993—resulted in the fiery deaths of seventy-two members of the millenarian religious sect as their compound burned to the ground. Dees pointed toward right-wing militia groups as the likely perpetrators of the bombing, arguing that many of the groups had been formed out of anger over the Waco incident and paranoia about the possibility of similar government law enforcement actions in the future. But McVeigh denies being affiliated with these militia groups. And members and supporters of the militia groups deny any involvement in the Oklahoma City bombing.

For several months prior to the Oklahoma City bombing, antiracist groups such as the SPLC and the Anti-Defamation League (ADL) warned of the danger that the militias represented. Chip Berlet of Political Research Associates reports that many of these groups expected violence to occur on April 19, given the significance of the Waco anniversary to the militias. According to Berlet, the militias are the militant armed wing of the "Patriot" movement, which is virulently antigovernment and vehemently opposed in particular to taxes, environmental regulations, federal gun control, and federal law enforcement authority. The militias tout the rights of gun owners, landowners, and the states as expressed in the Bill of Rights, Berlet maintains, and many of their members adhere to conspiracy theories concerning the role of the federal government in international affairs, in banking, and in the enforcement of civil rights laws. Berlet points out that the conspiracy theories and states' rights arguments that the militias profess are based on centuries-old anti-Semitic conspiracy theories and the arguments of southern states that opposed the abolition of slavery and

Militias Throughout the United States: June 1995

Source: *Klanwatch Intelligence Report*, June 1995.

resisted civil rights legislation. He contends that long-standing racist organizations such as the Ku Klux Klan (which began as a militia in the post–Civil War era) and the Aryan Nations are attempting to influence the militias with their ideologies. He also argues that these racist organizations are exploiting the militia members' suspicion of the federal government in order to foment antigovernment violence. For Berlet, the ADL, and the SPLC, the Oklahoma City bombing was a natural outgrowth of the influence of these racist organizations on the formation of the militias.

Members and supporters of the militias, however, argue that reports by groups such as the Southern Poverty Law Center and Anti-Defamation League grossly mischaracterize the aims of the militias. Mack Tanner, an Idaho-based reporter and writer, argues that the militias "are driven not by hatred of blacks or Jews or even the government" but by legitimate fears of attacks by federal law enforcement officials, such as the one that occurred at Waco. Tanner protests that the militias are clearly distinguishable from the criminal racists, violent radicals, and illegal tax protesters that the SPLC and others associate with them. He maintains that the militias are composed of "people who respect and obey the law" but who nevertheless fear that the government is trying to curtail their rights and freedoms. High on the militias' list of endangered freedoms is the right to keep and bear arms, according to Tanner, because members believe that this right guarantees all others. If citizens are armed and organized, militia members argue, then it is much harder for the federal government to encroach upon their rights. Far from promoting violence against the government, Tanner contends, being armed and organized tends to assuage the antigovernment fears of the militia members. And the militias keep a tight rein on their members, say the organizers. Bob Clarke, a Michigan Militia member, asserts that "if anyone starts talking nonsense that smacks of sedition or illegal attacks on the government, we kick them out." Tanner blames the SPLC and ADL for raising unjustified fears about the militias in the wake of the Oklahoma bombing. He maintains that the militias had nothing to do with the act of terrorism.

In a July 1995 interview in *Newsweek* magazine, Timothy McVeigh flatly denied that he is a member of a militia or that he ever attended any militia organizing meetings. But analysts at the SPLC maintain that the climate of fear and suspicion of government within these groups, as well as the racism promoted by certain organizers, inspired the bombing and create conditions that may lead to further violence. The viewpoints in the following chapter debate the role played by various groups in promoting antigovernment terrorism.

Citizen Militias Pose a Threat

by Loretta J. Ross

About the author: *Loretta J. Ross is the research director of the Center for Democratic Renewal in Atlanta, Georgia.*

The bombing of the federal building in Oklahoma City on April 19, 1995, was no isolated incident. Extremist right-wing groups around the country have been getting bigger and bolder for some time. While militia leaders are scrambling to distance themselves from Oklahoma, these groups pose a serious threat to our society.

They have been known to force confrontations with local sheriffs and have threatened to lynch any elected official they believe is a traitor. Attorney General Janet Reno, in particular, has been vilified by these people, and her personal security should be sharply increased.

These groups are dead serious about avenging Waco, which they viewed as a direct threat to them. White supremacists quickly rallied to support the Branch Davidians against the federal government. Many visited Waco during the siege. After the Waco disaster on April 19, 1993, hundreds of white supremacists and militia members made pilgrimages there, vowing revenge. It has become their Mecca, their Alamo.

That's why I wasn't surprised by the bombing. We were warned that something big might happen on April 19 to commemorate the anniversary of Waco. Several of the hatelines operated by white supremacists and militia groups announced that April 19 would be a "Day of Remembrance." It was also advertised in the pages of *Spotlight*, a racist and anti-Semitic newspaper published out of Washington. D.C., with approximately 125,000 subscribers.

The Militias' Agenda

Militias have been around since the Civil War in the form of the Ku Klux Klan, but their current popularity is a new phenomenon. The resurgence of the militias dates from the August 1992 siege of Randy Weaver's compound in

Loretta J. Ross, "Saying It with a Gun," *The Progressive*, June 1995. Reprinted with permission from *The Progressive*, 409 E. Main St., Madison, WI 53703.

Idaho, provoked by Weaver's weapons violations. During the ten-day standoff, agents from the Bureau of Alcohol, Tobacco and Firearms killed Weaver's wife and son. A federal marshal was also killed. Weaver's trial (he was acquitted of the murder of the federal marshal but convicted on the original weapons violations) sparked a frenzy of organizing by white supremacists, who pointed to his case as a symbol of government abuse.

Two months after the Weaver siege, Pete Peters of the Christian Identity movement organized a closed-door meeting in the Rocky Mountains attended by 150 leaders of different far-right groups. Militia activists developed a two-pronged strategy.

First, they had to build a national network of activists, supporters, resources, and information, with the goal of launching militia activities in all fifty states. Second, they had to be ready to deny what they were up to, so they identify themselves publicly as "unorganized militias," or uncoordinated groups of citizens independent of each other.

> *"While militia leaders are scrambling to distance themselves from Oklahoma, these groups pose a serious threat to our society."*

The second part of the strategy is obvious in the aftermath of the Oklahoma bombing. All of the militia spokesmen have denied having any connection with each other or the suspect arrested in the bombing.

This is critical because many of the militias' activities are criminally treasonous. They are attempting to form a citizens' army to overthrow the United States government. And they are acting in violation of laws against paramilitary activity in twenty-four states. They also engage in phony financial schemes and possibly gun-running to finance their movement.

Through a concept called "Leaderless Resistance," promoted by former Klansman Louis Beam, small, secretive cells of six to eight people are kept ignorant of each other, so that if one group is arrested, they cannot lead authorities to others. The cells commit the criminal activity and are unknown to the vast majority of the membership.

Some militia members are more openly racist and anti-Semitic, while others may be simply extremist patriots. What unites them, however, is their belief that peaceful democratic processes are not a viable solution.

They prefer to say it with a gun. They are also united by some bizarre conspiracy theories, which include that the United States is at risk of invasion by the United Nations; that the federal government is aiding and abetting this invasion; and that citizens, unless armed, will be rounded up and herded into concentration camps if they disagree with the government.

Help from Elected Officials

Elected officials associated with the militias have helped their cause. Representatives Helen Chenoweth, Republican of Idaho, Robert Dornan, Republican of California, Karen Thurman, Democrat of Florida, Mac Collins, Republican of Georgia, and James Hansen, Republican of Utah, as well as Senators Larry Craig, Republican of Utah, and Lauch Faircloth, Republican of North Carolina, have sent letters to the Justice Department or other agencies detailing the concerns of militia groups.

Colorado State Senator Charles Duke, California State Representative Don Rogers, and Georgia State Senator Pam Glanton spoke at a Georgia militia convention in March 1995. Duke has used his political platform to become a leader of the national Patriot movement. Calling himself a "state representative and a part-time revolutionary," Duke spoke at a Constitutionalist convention in Colorado, saying citizen militias are prepared to fight U.N. troops on Colorado soil. To militia members, armed confrontation with the government is inevitable. In the wake of the

> *"[The militias] are attempting to form a citizens' army to overthrow the United States government."*

bombing, they will probably lose some supporters and gain others. Some of their "softer" members—those not committed to the violent agenda—will quit the movement. More hard-core extremists are likely to refill the ranks with new recruits from the white-supremacist movement.

There will be further violence. Several militia leaders want to provoke a confrontation with law enforcement. Many do not pay their taxes and barricade themselves in fortresses, tactics guaranteed to bring government attention to them.

Unless we treat the growth of the far right as a serious problem, enforce laws against paramilitary activity that are already on the books, and counter inflammatory rhetoric, the Oklahoma City bombing may he seen by future generations as a beginning, not an end.

Citizen Militias Are a Response to Government Abuse of Power

by Alan W. Bock

About the author: *Alan W. Bock is senior columnist for the* Orange County Register, *a newspaper published in Orange County, California. He is the author of the book* Ambush at Ruby Ridge.

Before the April 1995 bombing in Oklahoma City the "citizens' militias" that have cropped up throughout the country in recent years had a reputation as harmless nuts with a penchant for paranoia and kooky conspiracy theories. Now they are widely seen as a serious threat to public order and safety.

The Bombing Suspects and the Militias

The transformation from wacky to dangerous was triggered by alleged links between the militia movement and suspects in the Oklahoma City bombing. The evidence of these links so far is fragmentary and uncertain. Early press accounts reported that Timothy McVeigh, the young Army veteran charged in the case, was affiliated with the Michigan Militia. James and Terry Nichols, two brothers who are friends of McVeigh (Terry Nichols has been charged in the case), were said to have attended militia meetings.

But leaders of the Michigan Militia, which was officially founded in April 1994 and claims a membership of 12,000 statewide, say neither Timothy McVeigh nor the Nichols brothers are members of their organization. They say James Nichols, perhaps with his brother, came to one of the organization's public meetings but was asked to leave after he urged those attending to tear up their driver's licenses and stop paying taxes. The Militia of Montana (MOM) reports that none of the three men's names appears in the databases listing militia members and sympathizers around the country. So the preliminary evidence suggests that if McVeigh and the Nichols brothers had a connection with the militia movement, it was as troublesome sympathizers rather than actual members.

Still, many people who share some of the militia movement's dislike of an increasingly intrusive Federal Government are disturbed by the idea of private armed groups engaging in organized military training. They may remember references to the role of the militias in the War of Independence, and they know that the word appears in the Second Amendment, which guarantees the right to keep and bear arms, but in terms that do not make absolutely clear whether the right is individual or corporate. But to many Americans the militia seems an archaic concept, out of place in a world of nuclear weapons and cruise missiles. Why has this concept been revived in the last few years, and why has it resonated with so many people?

The Weaver and Waco Raids

The short answer is: Weaver, Waco, and Brady. To many Americans, that list symbolizes a Federal Government intent on preparing us for a New World Order in which U.S. sovereignty will be subordinated to the United Nations (UN) (or some successor organization) and our constitutional rights will cease to exist. Federal officials argue that the popular accounts of Weaver and Waco are grossly exaggerated. And it's certainly true that these sorts of violent raids mostly appear to result from ineptitude, headline seeking, individual abuse of authority, or bureaucratic competition. But if it is hard to justify the militias' claim that these actions are part of some New World Order conspiracy, it is equally hard to justify the government's actions as the proper execution of legitimate authority.

Randy Weaver, a white separatist who lived in a secluded cabin in northern Idaho, was entrapped on a sawed-off-shotgun charge by the Bureau of Alcohol, Tobacco, and Firearms, which then asked him to become a BATF spy within the racist Aryan Nation. He refused and was indicted. After Weaver failed to appear in court on the firearms charge, the Federal Government set up an elaborate eighteen-month surveillance operation that culminated on August 21, 1992, in a gun battle in which Weaver's fourteen-year-old son and a

> *"The evidence of these links [between the militia movement and the Oklahoma City bombing suspects] so far is fragmentary and uncertain."*

federal marshal were killed. During the ensuing eleven-day standoff, Weaver's wife, Vicki, was killed, and Randy Weaver and his friend Kevin Harris were wounded. In the federal trial that followed, Weaver was acquitted of all charges except the failure-to-appear count. No charges have been brought in the deaths of his wife and son, but the local prosecutor is still investigating, and Weaver himself has brought a civil suit [which was settled out of court].

On April 19, 1993, while the Weaver trial was taking place, the Branch Davidian compound near Waco, Texas, burned to the ground during an assault by federal agents. The assault followed an initial BATF raid in February 1993 based on defective search and arrest warrants stemming from firearms charges. It left more than eighty people dead, including more than two dozen children.

Gun-Control Laws

It is, however, the Clinton Administration's success in 1994 in passing the Brady Bill, requiring a waiting period for handgun purchases, and the more recent ban on "assault weapons" that make these violent confrontations seem less like the actions of rogue elements within particular agencies and more like part of a general effort by the Federal Government to remove all firearms from private hands. Certainly there are plenty of gun-control advocates who would like to see universal gun registration as a way-station toward an ultimate ban on the private ownership of firearms. In 1991, at a B'nai B'rith meeting in Fort Lauderdale, Florida, Janet Reno, then chief state prosecutor in Dade County, declared that "the most effective means of fighting crime in the United States is to outlaw the possession of any type of firearm by the civilian populace." Many people in positions of power share that view.

> *"It is . . . hard to justify the government's actions [in the Weaver and Waco cases] as the proper execution of legitimate authority."*

Miss Reno and others have defended the Weaver and Waco raids as instances of the government protecting other citizens from armed and dangerous extremists. But there have been a disturbing number of assaults by federal agents in recent years—resulting in lost property, damaged reputations, and occasional deaths—in which there was not even that justification. On October 2, 1992, Donald Scott, a reclusive millionaire in Malibu, California, was killed in an early-morning police raid apparently perpetrated with the intent of seizing his property under federal forfeiture law. The police had received a tip that Scott was growing marijuana; no plants were found. On May 6, 1992, a health clinic in Washington State was raided by armed agents of the Food and Drug Administration, who confiscated contraband vitamin B-12. Agents of the most unlikely federal agencies—the Bureau of Land Management, the Environmental Protection Agency, the Internal Revenue Service, the Immigration and Naturalization Service, the Forest Service—have taken to enforcing regulations with armed officers, sometimes in full combat regalia, often through surprise raids conducted in cooperation with local law-enforcement agencies. No federal agents have been tried or even indicted for any of the civilian deaths resulting from these paramilitary excursions. . . .

The New Militias

In the early 1990s numerous groups calling themselves citizens' militias sprang up. They range from what are essentially civic organizations that do a little organized target practice on weekends to paramilitary groups led by people worried about the possibility that a master plan exists to subvert U.S. sovereignty, snatch the people's guns, and impose a UN-directed dictatorship. Some militia organizations hold their meetings openly, advertising in newspapers and welcoming all comers, while others are secretive. A few militia leaders associate or sympathize with racist groups, and racist and anti-Semitic organizers certainly see the militia movement as a recruiting opportunity. Many militia leaders, in turn, have gone out of their way to expel or otherwise dissociate themselves from people who seem to be animated by racist sentiments.

How many people are connected with some form of militia? Estimates range from ten thousand to millions. The true figure for members actively engaged in training is probably in the tens of thousands. In October 1994, the Anti-Defamation League of B'nai B'rith issued a report titled "Armed and Dangerous: Militias Take Aim at the Federal Government," outlining recent militia activity in thirteen states. More recent 1995 estimates indicate that militia groups are active in at least thirty-five states and perhaps in all fifty by now; California alone has a dozen local groups. The militia groups have used fax networks and the Internet to get information to a large number of interested people in a short time, but the movement is decentralized. Some groups are strictly local, while others stay in contact with likeminded organizations elsewhere.

> *"The most unlikely federal agencies . . . have taken to enforcing regulations with armed officers, sometimes in full combat regalia."*

Most organizers stress the militias' essentially defensive character. John Trochmann is co-organizer of the Militia of Montana, which regularly attracts hundreds of people to informational meetings and is considered one of the most radical organized militias. Trochmann claims that the purpose of organizing the militia was not to provoke but rather to defuse confrontations like the Randy Weaver standoff. He says MOM is in regular contact with Federal Bureau of Investigation (FBI) and BATF agents as well as with local sheriffs and elected officials. And although Trochmann, along with several other MOM members, was recently arrested in Roundup, Montana, on charges of threatening government officials, it turned out to be a misunderstanding, and the charges were dropped.

The Well-Regulated Militia and Illegal Activity

The apparently well-organized Michigan Militia, which claims 12,000 members, has condemned the Oklahoma City bombing and stressed that neither McVeigh nor the Nichols brothers are members. Leaders of the militia say they do not countenance illegal activity. An incident in August 1994 illustrates some of the tensions. Three men in camouflage uniforms and with numerous weapons in their car were arrested at a late-night traffic stop in Fowlerville, Michigan, and released on bail. They didn't show up for their arraignment, but some thirty people claiming to be militia members did, taunting, insulting, and threatening the police. Michigan Militia Commander Norman Olson disavowed these people, saying they were part of an "underground group" and not militia members.

"We are a 'well-regulated' militia and will not let our people break the laws," Olson says. "Members are under strict orders not to carry weapons. We use the same procedures and regulations as the military."

That may be true of some organized militias, but is it true of all? And could the rhetoric and tactics used to recruit militia members inspire breakaway groups or loose cannons to initiate violence? On videotapes and in speeches around the country, militia leader Mark Koernke, a/k/a "Mark from Michigan," sounds calm and measured. But he also sounds quite certain that Multi-Jurisdictional Task Forces, the Financial Crimes Enforcement Network, the black helicopters seen near military bases, and foreign troops training in the U.S.—as well as the Weaver and Waco killings and new gun-control laws—are part of a well-orchestrated plan to steal American freedom and place the U.S. under UN control. He seems sure that new outrages are imminent and that action is needed *now* to avert the threat. It's not hard to imagine unstable people listening, absorbing, and deciding to do something crazy.

Legal Questions

There are also questions about the legal status of militias that resemble private armies. Most states have laws against organized armed groups operating without state sanction, and most citizens' militias, even those that have sought communication and cooperation with law-enforcement agencies, have steered clear of affiliation with state governments. Some advocates say the right to form a militia is based on the constitutional rights to peaceably assemble and to keep and bear arms. But the constitutional provisions and laws concerning militias refer to the whole of the people, subject to call-up by duly constituted authorities. They do not license private armies. And there is a certain tension between the militia's role as a check on the government and its role as a force for the government to direct in emergencies.

Furthermore, a militia that claims to represent the whole people should theoretically be open to membership for anyone who chooses to volunteer. Yet most militia groups reserve the right to exclude people who sound too radical or who are suspected of being undercover agents. Does that make them simply private organizations with no real right to call themselves militias and to partake in the tradition the word implies?

> *"The purpose of organizing the militia was not to provoke but rather to defuse confrontations like the Randy Weaver standoff."*

The militia movement has the potential to provoke violent confrontations. But it has arisen, at least in part, in response to violent confrontations in which federal law-enforcement agencies seem to have abused their powers. The best way to defuse the movement would surely be a serious congressional investigation of Waco, Weaver, and other incidents, followed by appropriate action—i.e., curbing federal agencies that overstep constitutional and statutory boundaries.

Before the Oklahoma City bombing, it seemed possible that Congress would do so. Hearings were scheduled to investigate abuses by the BATF and other agencies, and it seemed possible that Congress would vote to repeal the Brady Bill and the assault-weapons ban. In the wake of the bombing, the gun-control votes have been put on hold [while hearings on Weaver and Waco have gone forward]. Republicans and Democrats have fallen all over one another in their eagerness to beef up the jurisdiction, power, numbers, and funding of the FBI and BATF. Yet giving the agencies that frighten so many Americans even more power hardly seems like a rational response—even to a sometimes irrational movement.

The Political Right Promotes Terrorist Violence

by Kent Worcester

About the author: *Kent Worcester is a member of the editorial board of* New Politics, *a socialist journal, and author of* C.L.R. James: A Political Biography *and* Trade Union Politics: American Unions and Economic Change, 1960s–1990s.

The carnage of the April 1995 Oklahoma bombing puts a new spin on what has been called the politics of rage. Before Oklahoma, the most visible expression of the country's march to the right was the construction of a hard Republican majority in Congress in the November 1994 elections. In the wake of Oklahoma, the putschist fantasies of a radical, sometimes "revolutionary" right have come into sharper focus. The bombing not only highlights the dangers posed by domestic neo-fascists, but raises questions about the porous borders dividing mainstream conservatives from the radical fringe. For this reason, the potential significance of Oklahoma is that it represents a rare opportunity to recast the terms of political debate.

The Bombing and Radical Right Beliefs

The paramilitary unit that took out the main federal building in Oklahoma City on April 19, 1995, had its sights trained, not only on federal agencies, but also on public employees, their children, and passersby whose only connection was their physical proximity. (The fact that many federal employees are African-American or Hispanic is unlikely to have escaped their attention.) The bombers were almost certainly inspired by the Aryan tract *The Turner Diaries*, which recounts the activities of a racist organization that detonates an ammonium nitrate fertilizer bomb in front of the Federal Bureau of Investigation (FBI) headquarters just after 9 a.m. The Order, as they call themselves, intend for the bomb to serve as a wake-up call to white America—and they succeed, to the point of turning most of the country into a charnel house.

The Turner Diaries offers a particularly grisly example of what has become a genre of books, tapes, tactical manuals, and so on, denouncing the feds, railing against "enemies within," and calling for a "second violent American revolution." Virulent strains of right-wing thought have always enjoyed a presence in American life, but reactionary propaganda has found an especially appreciative audience in the last ten to fifteen years, and particularly since the Democrats recaptured the White House in 1992. Two events—the immolation of the Branch Davidian compound in 1993, and the siege of the home of tax resister Randy Weaver a year earlier [in August 1992]—have heightened rightist anxieties about an imminent government takeover of arms and private property.

The Structure of the Radical Right

The radical right is comprised of an embattled subculture of fundamentalists and conspiracists conjoined by the usual litany of grievances. Most conservatives broadly sympathize with many of their concerns, but distrust their new world order paranoia and malevolent rhetoric. Radical rightists are also tied together by newspapers (*Spotlight, Human Events*), organizations (Klan groups, Aryan sects, Reconstructionist ministries), and informal media (fax, internet, shortwave radio). The information age has facilitated greater international outreach, while permissive gun laws have allowed racist groups (and extreme anti-abortion groups) to stockpile guns, ammo, and explosives.

The militias are a recent innovation, concocted by savvy political entrepreneurs who have launched themselves as saviors of the Second Amendment with the aid of armed camps of weekend warriors. They provide a context where enraged gun-nuts and credulous Ditto-heads [Rush Limbaugh fans] can be inducted into an explicitly racist and supremacist milieu. As a war veteran and foot soldier in the army of white supremacy, Timothy

> *"The bombing ... raises questions about the porous borders dividing mainstream conservatives from the radical fringe."*

McVeigh [who is charged in the Oklahoma bombing] attached himself to the militia movement, selling weapons, exchanging information, and gaining reassurance that a massive confrontation was indeed brewing between "patriotic Americans" and an illegitimate state.

What does all of this obsessive madness have to do with today's triumphant conservatism? Absolutely nothing, to judge by responses to Clinton's timid suggestion that "purveyors of hatred and division" fostered a climate that helped facilitate the Oklahoma bombing. George Will found the president's words "contemptible." William Safire said that Clinton was indulging in a "form of extremism." Rush Limbaugh blamed liberals for whipping up "national hysteria." Newt Gingrich, for his part, said that efforts to link his self-proclaimed "revolution" with the Oklahoma bombing were "grotesque and offensive." For these critics, the perpetrators of the Oklahoma attack are merely lawbreakers. "Responsibility rests on the criminals themselves," intoned Safire, "not on chosen motivators or 'root causes.'"

A more common response has been to attack "extremists on both sides." In this spirit, Jacob Weisberg, in *New York* magazine [May 8, 1995], drew parallels between McVeigh and the Weather Underground [terrorist faction of Students for a Democratic Society in the 1960s and 1970s], and Newt Gingrich and Leonard Bernstein, who hosted a 1970 fundraising benefit for the Black Panthers. Several pundits played up the fact that the northern Californian wood-fetishist Unabomber killed his third victim within hours of the Oklahoma disaster. After chiding the hard right in his *New York Times* column, A.M. Rosenthal lashed out at his real targets—"intellectuals of the movie business who make big money portraying America as viciously as any militiaman . . . lobbyists who cry out that if antiterrorism is tightened, hundreds of thousands of Arab-Americans will be dragged off to concentration camps . . . [and] the campus Bullies for Hatred across the country."

The Radical Right and More "Respectable" Conservatives

Just as this hysteria was reaching a high-pitched crescendo, fresh revelations emerged about the real world co-mingling of the radical fringe and more respectable elements. It turned out, for example, that at least two new members of Congress, Helen Chenoweth (Idaho) and Steve Stockman (Texas), are aligned with the militia movement. The Militia of Montana, led by former members of the Aryan Nation, merchandise a video in which Chenoweth explains that more than 50 percent of the United States is under "the control of the New World Order." Along with Stockman and Chenoweth, Senators Lauch Faircloth (North Carolina) and Larry Craig (Idaho), wrote militia-inspired letters to Janet Reno prior to the bombing to complain that nefarious agents of a one-world dictatorship were mobilizing troops and black helicopters against ordinary citizens. Reports have also come out about radio call-in hosts who incite listeners to engage in acts of violence against liberals and public officials. Chuck Baker, Bob Mohan, and other talk show personalities provide listeners with the addresses and phone numbers of radical right groups. G. Gordon Liddy, said to be the nation's second most popular talk show host, gleefully offers on-air suggestions about how to inflict maximum damage against political targets. Newt Gingrich, Bob Dole, Phil Gramm, and others have been regular guests on Liddy's show.

> *"Most conservatives broadly sympathize with many of [the radical right's] concerns."*

The bombing has brought to light a dense network of racist activists working to restrict immigration, fight gun control, illegalize abortion, and combat federal tyranny. One columnist cited the example of Lawrence Pratt, who heads both Gun Owners of America and the Committee to Protect the Family Foundation, a fund-raising front for Operation Rescue. Pratt regularly speaks alongside Mark Koernke, the notorious leader of the Michigan Militia, and funnels money into the coffers of House member Steve Stockman and other friends of the movement. One of Pratt's collaborators is the survivalist guru Bo Gritz, who characterized the Oklahoma bombing as "a Rembrandt—a masterpiece of science and art put together." While these people are not as well known as, say, Jesse Helms or Robert Dornan, their strategy of "leaderless resistance" resonates more effectively in some quarters than either Jack Kemp's opportunity conservatism or Gingrich's crackpot futurism.

The Radical Right and Conservative Causes

At the local level, there are a number of causes that blur the distinction between conservatism and right-wing radicalism. One is the anti–gun control movement, led by the National Rifle Association, which has extensive ties to the militia movement. Another is the Wise Use movement, which views private property as sacred and opposes all forms of land use planning. The most significant, perhaps, is the anti-abortion movement. From the 1980s on, militant anti-abortionists have engaged in numerous acts of arson, bombing, intolerable harassment of clinic workers, and even murder. While each of these movements contains a wide range of activists—most of whom were appalled by the Oklahoma bombing—each offers critical points of contact between grassroots conservatism and the radical right.

"The tragedy of Oklahoma is that it took an act of mass murder to show that the right is infested with homicidal crazies."

Another key point of contact is the Christian Coalition of Pat Robertson and Ralph Reed, which is currently amassing power within the Republican Party. Fueled by Robertson's theories of a New World Order headed by financiers (who happen to be Jews), the Christian Coalition is working overtime to transform the country into a strait-jacketed theocracy.

The tragedy of Oklahoma is that it took an act of mass murder to show that the right is infested with homicidal crazies who want to turn Patrick Buchanan's "culture war" into a bloodbath. Even now, most pundits, as well as Clinton and the Democrats, view Oklahoma as an aberration, or an opportunity to roll back individual liberties through counter-terrorism measures. The sad fact is that Oklahoma was exceptional only in terms of scale. Placed in the context of escalating levels of anti-abortion clinic violence, and the emergence of a militia movement that has effectively tapped into the politics of vengeance, Oklahoma becomes a potent symbol of the right's capacity to engage in acts of unspeakable barbarism.

The Federal Government Provokes Terrorism

by Doug Bandow

About the author: *Doug Bandow is a senior fellow at the Cato Institute, a libertarian think tank in Washington, D.C.*

Washington is often convulsed by events that have no impact on the rest of America. Not so the April 1995 Oklahoma City bombing, which, in contrast to so many other actions, dominated nation and capital alike. And understandably so. It is impossible to describe adequately the horror of the terrorist attack, though many people have tried. The picture of bloodied children alone is enough to indelibly imprint upon our society the barbarity of terrorism, with its helpless, innocent victims.

The Reactions of Politicians and People

Yet if it seemed like ruled and rulers could come together for one moment, it was only one brief moment. Unfortunately, the reactions in and out of Washington were completely different. Around the country was anger, desire for understanding, and hope for healing. In the halls of the White House and Congress was shock, followed by a race for political advantage and demand for more power. In short, everyone did what comes most naturally to them—citizens worried about their countrymen while politicians worried about their influence.

Consider first the attempt to brand critics of government as contributing to a "climate of hate" in which violence might occur. Needless to say, it is in the interest of presidents, legislators, and bureaucrats alike to discourage criticism. And many have been quick to use the tragedy in Oklahoma City in an attempt to place themselves beyond reproach.

For instance, the American Federation of State, County, and Municipal Employees (AFSCME) ran an ad in the *New York Times* titled "The Call of Duty." AFSCME argued that "the people who work in government service are the faces of America. Serving all of us." Thus, continued the union, "Isn't it time to end the constant attacks on the people who serve us? Who knows what the

Doug Bandow, "Terror: Against or by Government?" *Freeman*, August 1995. Reprinted with permission of the author.

twisted mind of a terrorist might think? *Or do.*" Ah, if only the *Freeman* hadn't been criticizing failed government programs for decades, the Oklahoma City bombing might never have occurred.

Aside from the fact that this argument is both nonsensical and self-serving, it is also, well, dangerous. What is more likely to create a climate of hate—denouncing illegal and unconstitutional practices by the State that are harmful and sometimes deadly, or covering up such practices and denouncing the people who point them out? It is, in a sense, the new McCarthyism—criticize government, and you are accused of being an accessory to terrorism.

The Real Cause of Terrorism

Indeed, this kind of finger-pointing will make it harder to address the real causes of terrorism. Criticism of government does not occur in a vacuum. More than half of respondents in a 1995 Gallup poll say they fear for "the rights and freedoms of ordinary citizens" at the hands of the federal government. And they do so for a reason.

This is where Washington is so very far out of touch. Most policymakers honestly don't understand why anyone would criticize, let alone fear them. Their sentiment was captured by historian Alan Brinkley who, in an article in the *American Prospect*, asked: "How has it happened that among all the powerful institutions in modern society, government has become the principal, often even the only, target of opprobrium among Americans angry and frustrated about their lack of control over their lives?"

How? Ask Randy Weaver, whose family was gunned down by Federal Bureau of Investigation (FBI) sharpshooters in Ruby Ridge, Idaho, in August 1992. Ask the parents of the Branch Davidian children who were burned alive in Waco, Texas, in the midst of a Bureau of Alcohol, Tobacco and Firearms (BATF) assault in April 1993. Ask Mary Williams, whose seventy-five-year-old husband died of a heart attack during a mistaken SWAT team drug raid on their apartment in Boston. Ask Donald Carlson, who was shot three times in a faulty Drug Enforcement Administration (DEA) raid on his home in Poway, California. Ask the thousands upon thousands of people who've had land seized by the Environmental Protection Agency, been audited by the Internal Revenue Service (IRS), and been otherwise harassed by the government.

"It is, in a sense, the new McCarthyism—criticize government, and you are accused of being an accessory to terrorism."

Someone needs to explain to Professor Brinkley that only the government can seize property and kill people with relative impunity. Only the government can destroy businesses, level homes, impose taxes, and regulate property with minimal restraint. Only the government has a monopoly of force. Only the government warrants constant suspicion and fear.

The Government's Role in Promoting Terrorism

The fact that the State has enormous power and has constantly misused that power requires us, especially in the aftermath of the Oklahoma City attack, to talk about the unsavory role of the U.S. government in promoting terrorism. Although nothing could ever justify Oklahoma City, it, along with other murderous assaults, like the February 1993 World Trade Center bombing, should not surprise us. Unfortunately, the United States has spent years creating and inflaming a multitude of grievances here and abroad, grievances that some misguided people believe can be resolved only through violence and murder.

For instance, the Oklahoma City bombing may have been a bizarre retaliation for the destruction of the Branch Davidian compound in Waco two years before. Only a twisted mind could think that the killing of four-score people by the government warranted the slaughter of nearly 170 people in and around a government building. Nevertheless, no one should doubt that Waco, too, was terrorism, only committed by the federal government. Neither the absurdity of David Koresh and his beliefs nor the convoluted legal allegations against him justified the initial raid, let alone the final assault. Apparently only the government can risk children's lives with impunity.

The World Trade Center bombing, too, was a predictable outgrowth of official U.S. policy. Persistent American intervention in the Middle East alone has been enough to turn the United States into an international target of terrorism. Though murderously misdirected and morally monstrous, the attacks are a natural response to Washington's determination to make everyone else's international conflicts its own by continually meddling in foreign squabbles and seemingly condoning most any injustice perpetrated by most any ally.

The Government's Antagonism Toward Muslims

Consider the 1983 bombing of the Marine Corps barracks in Lebanon. The United States sent soldiers into the middle of a civil war, sided with one of the warring parties, and shelled Muslim villages as a show of strength. How, then, could anyone have been surprised when a suicide bomber reversed the direction of death, making 241 young Marines pay the supreme price? The United States intervened in a distant conflict for no cause and terrorized peoples with whom it had no quarrel,

> *"Only the government has a monopoly on force. Only the government warrants constant suspicion and fear."*

providing everything but an engraved invitation to revenge-minded killers. Unfortunately, American policymakers should share responsibility with foreign terrorists for the soldiers' deaths.

Especially dangerous today is the government's campaign to make an enemy of every living Muslim fundamentalist, wherever he resides in the world. There's no doubt that Islam poses a serious challenge to Western culture and values. But the

United States can do little to halt its spread and has no reason to intentionally antagonize Muslims who otherwise wouldn't even think about America. Yet Washington is speaking of alliances with African nations that most policymakers, let alone citizens, can't find on a map, in order to "contain" an ancient religion that has endured for centuries. Declaring a de facto war on Islam invites retaliation, and the most likely victims will be innocent Americans.

> *"No one should doubt that Waco, too, was terrorism, only committed by the federal government."*

Yes, the United States must respond to terrorism. Part of the solution is improved detection, prevention, and punishment. But the United States must also reduce the manifold justifications, perverse and warped though they be, for terrorism that it has needlessly provided to those with seared consciences and murderous intentions. There are many good reasons why people both fear and criticize government. So long as Washington tolerates, encourages, and, worse, engages in one or another variant of terrorism, it will risk repetitions not only of Oklahoma City, but also of the plethora of other bloody attacks around the globe in recent years.

Islamic Terrorists Pose a Threat

by James Phillips

About the author: *James Phillips is a senior policy analyst with the Heritage Foundation, a conservative public policy foundation in Washington, D.C.*

The February 26, 1993, bombing of the World Trade Center in New York City was a curious terrorist operation. On the one hand it was well-planned and professional; the terrorists were able secretly to construct and deploy a massive truck bomb. On the other hand, it was a surprisingly amateurish operation. The four terrorists convicted of the attack took unnecessary risks, such as giving a correct name and address when renting a vehicle for delivering the bomb.

Possible Foreign Sponsors

So far, no foreign state has been found responsible for the World Trade Center attack. But there are disturbing shreds of circumstantial evidence that point to possible Iranian or Iraqi involvement. Sheik Omar Abdul Rahman, the radical Egyptian cleric who inspired and possibly directed the bombers, long has been on the Iranian payroll, according to Vincent Cannistraro, the former head of Central Intelligence Agency (CIA) counterterrorism operations. Sheik Omar regularly was given large sums of money by Iran's intelligence service, using Iran's delegation to the United Nations as a conduit. U.S. government investigators discovered that about $100,000 was transferred to the suspects before the bombing from banks in foreign countries, including Iran, but it is not known if this was payment for the attack or for other activities such as propaganda or recruitment.

Other signs point toward Iraq. For instance, the attack took place during the second anniversary of the ground offensive against Iraq in Operation Desert Storm. Terrorist attacks launched on anniversaries historically have been a common means of seeking vengeance in the Middle East. Another troubling circumstance is that Ramzi Yousef, who apparently set the plot in motion, entered the U.S. in 1992 on an Iraqi passport on a trip that began in Iraq. Moreover, Abdul Yasin, an Iraqi suspect who cooperated with the Federal Bureau of Investi-

Excerpted from James Phillips, "The Changing Face of Middle Eastern Terrorism," *Backgrounder* no. 1005, October 6, 1994. Reprinted by permission of The Heritage Foundation.

gation (FBI) and was released from jail, later flew back to Iraq and is now believed to be living in Baghdad. Many New York law enforcement officials reportedly believe that Iraq was involved, although they cannot prove it.

Iraq also would seem to have more to gain from such a terrorist operation than Iran. Saddam Hussein would have had a strong incentive to punish the U.S. for its role in Desert Storm. Iraq also may have wanted to provoke a confrontation between the U.S. and its arch-rival Iran by casting suspicion on Tehran for the bombing. This would strengthen Iraq's perceived value in the Middle East as a bulwark against revolutionary Iran, an argument Iraqi diplomats have made in attempts to persuade members of the United Nations Security Council to lift the U.N.-mandated sanctions against Iraq.

A final disquieting consideration was the nature of the World Trade Center bomb itself. Not only was the bomb huge, loaded with 1,200 pounds of explosives, but it was customized with compressed hydrogen to magnify the blast and sodium cyanide to create a poisonous cloud after the explosion. A bomb that big and sophisticated has never before been detonated by a terrorist group that did not have state sponsorship or long-standing experience in building explosive devices.

The New Breed of Radical Islamic Terrorists

The World Trade Center bombers are a new breed of terrorist. Unlike the tightly disciplined cells that dominated terrorism in the past, they functioned in a loosely organized *ad hoc* manner. Three of the six charged with the bombing were dedicated followers of Sheik Omar Abdul Rahman, the fiery spiritual leader of the Islamic Group, a radical fundamentalist movement that has waged a terrorist campaign to overthrow the Egyptian government.

At least three of the six bombers had fought in the war in Afghanistan against Soviet and Afghan communists. The Sheik also made at least three visits there since 1980 and two of his sons reportedly fought there. Thousands of Muslims from roughly forty countries flocked to Afghanistan following the 1979 Soviet invasion. Radicalized veterans from the Afghan war—called by some journalists the "University of Jihad" (Holy War)—have returned home and have become the spearheads of radical Islamic movements in Algeria, Azerbaijan, Bosnia, Egypt, Sudan, and many other places around the world. Hundreds of these "Afghanis" are being trained by Iranian Revolutionary Guards in Sudanese training camps.

> *"The World Trade Center bombers are a new breed of terrorist."*

Radical Islamic Groups in the West

Radical Islamic movements have mushroomed not only in the Muslim world, but also among Muslim immigrants in the West. The World Trade Center bombers were all either recent immigrants or illegal aliens. Although they may have been drawn to America by economic opportunities and political freedoms, these terrorists rejected America's values and what they considered to be its degenerate culture of materialism and secularism. Rejecting assimilation into the resented society of their host country, they were susceptible to incitement by Sheik Omar. What they did mirrors what happened in several other terrorism cases, such as Hezbollah's 1985–1986 bombing campaign in France and its bombings in Buenos Aires, Argentina, in 1992 and 1994. In all three cases, small portions of local immigrant communities provided support for the terrorist operations.

Ironically, many radical Islamic movements outlawed in their own countries have found sanctuary in Western countries. So long as they are in the West, they cannot be arrested by the police back home. Like

> *"These potential terrorists are dangerous because . . . they are now blending into Western societies where they have established personal and communal roots."*

Sheik Omar, leaders of these radical movements lambaste their host countries while taking advantage of their open political systems to travel freely, organize politically, raise funds, recruit new members, support underground opposition movements in their home countries, and sometimes to direct terrorist activities. Germany long has been a base for Islamic extremists. The U.S. has become a safe haven for Hezbollah, the Islamic Group, Algerian fundamentalists, and Palestinian fundamentalists. Israeli officials claim that Hamas (Islamic Resistance Movement), the radical Palestinian Islamic group that is using terrorism to undermine the nascent Palestinian-Israeli peace, actually is directed from a headquarters in the United States.

The support networks that these terrorist groups are forming inside the U.S. for fund-raising, recruitment, and propaganda activities could become the nucleus for terrorist attacks on American soil. These potential terrorists are dangerous because, unlike hit teams dispatched from the Middle East, they are now blending into Western societies where they have established personal and communal roots. U.S. counterterrorism officials worry that "sleeper cells" already established inside the U.S. could lie dormant for many years until activated for specific terrorist actions.

Moreover, the decentralized structure of many of the radical Islamic movements makes it difficult for host governments to detect, defend against, or apprehend terrorists lurking within these movements. The loosely linked informal webs of Islamic militants, often organized in small groups around a charismatic cleric, are harder to track and infiltrate than the more rigidly organized Palestinian terrorist groups that have been a major threat for decades. The Palestinian groups had a more straightforward organization and often were corrupt and therefore susceptible to bribery. They also were easier to penetrate because infighting between rival organizations led them to provide information on each other.

Islamic Terrorists Oppose American Values

The new breed of radical Islamic terrorist is more intractable, less likely to betray other terrorists, and more unpredictable. In contrast to long-established Palestinian terrorist groups who had more predictable targets and objectives, Islamic radicals have more unclear motives and a wider variety of targets. They not only attack Israel, secular governments in Muslim countries, and states that support the secular regimes they oppose, they also target reporters with whom they disagree, intellectuals they despise (such as Salman Rushdie, the author of *The Satanic Verses*), and Western cultural institutions such as the American University in Beirut.

Most Palestinian terrorist groups refrained from assaulting Americans or launching attacks on American soil. The reason: they wanted to influence American public opinion to change U.S. foreign policy and to drive a wedge between Israel and America. They made the cold-blooded political calculation that killing Americans would hurt rather than help their political cause.

This self-imposed restraint often is not as strong among Islamic militants. This new breed of terrorist is hostile not only to American policies, but to many American values. For example, they reject secular law and democracy and the separation of church and state. They view American culture as a threat to Islamic piety and revile what they perceive to be the degenerate secular and materialist bias of American society. To Islamic radicals, the U.S. is the villainous successor of the European colonial empires that have sought to dominate the Middle East since the time of the crusades. In their holy war against the West, terrorism is an acceptable instrument for carrying out the will of God. Because they are motivated by apocalyptic zeal, and not sober political calculations, their choice of possible targets is much wider and more indiscriminate than that of other terrorists. Since they are less predictable, they can be more dangerous than Palestinian or other Middle Eastern terrorists.

> *"This new breed of terrorist is hostile not only to American policies, but to many American values."*

Islamic radicals also often have a different audience in mind than Palestinian nationalists. Instead of using terrorism to influence Western powers to change their policies, they often use terrorism to punish Western powers and inspire other Muslims to rise up against the West. This focus on the Muslim audience rather than an American audience helps explain how the bombers of the World Trade Center could rationalize their bloody actions. The bombing was meant to demonstrate the power of Islamic radicals and the vulnerability of the U.S., not to lead the U.S. to rethink its Middle East policy.

Muslims in America Are Not a Terrorist Threat

by Mohamed Nimer

About the author: *Mohamed Nimer is a political scientist specializing in Muslim and Middle East politics and is an independent consultant who has written research reports for the Council on American-Islamic Relations in Washington, D.C.*

In March 1994, a handful of militant Muslims were convicted in the February 1993 World Trade Center (WTC) bombing, leaving many questions in the minds of many Americans about the intentions of Muslims living in their midst. Some writers have sought to convince the public that there is a serious "Islamic terrorist threat to America." (See for example: Yossef Bodansky, *Target America: Terrorism in the U.S. Today,* 1993.) Was the WTC bombing just the beginning of an Islamic campaign of urban terrorism directed at U.S. cities? Are speculations about a Muslim terrorist threat in the United States reasonable?

The Myth of an Islamic Threat

Mainstream American leaders and officials have dismissed the notion that the Islamic revival constitutes a security threat to the United States. Even in the domain of foreign policy, American leaders stated that they do not envision a "global Islamic threat" to U.S. security. In a May 1994 speech delivered in Washington, DC, National Security Advisor Anthony Lake said, "We also reject the notion that a renewed emphasis on traditional values in the Islamic world must inevitably conflict with the West or with democratic principles."

The history of terrorism in the United States is not consistent with the mythical picture of "the Islamic terrorist threat on U.S. soil." According to government figures, radicals from Muslim backgrounds carried out only one terrorist attack in the United States—the World Trade Center bombing. In contrast, the following figures on the backgrounds of individuals who committed domestic terrorist attacks are reported by the Federal Bureau of Investigation (FBI) in the period 1982–1992: Puerto Ricans, seventy-seven attacks; left-wing groups,

Excerpted from Mohamed Nimer, "Muslims in the USA: A Religious Community, Not a Security Threat," a paper from the Council on American-Islamic Relations, Washington, D.C., revised by the author for inclusion in this volume.

twenty-three attacks; Jewish, sixteen attacks; anti-Castro Cubans, twelve attacks; right-wing groups, six attacks. Such information, however, does not warrant sweeping generalizations about the connection of ethnic communities or political ideologies to terrorism. Nor does the WTC bombing justify a correlation between Muslim activism and violence.

The Media Reaction to Oklahoma City

Still, some cling to stereotypical images of Muslims, who are often portrayed as "hotheaded fanatics bent on waging holy wars against infidels." After the April 19, 1995, bombing of Oklahoma City's Murrah Federal Building, media reporters and political pundits immediately pointed fingers at Muslims, accusing them of carrying out the bombing. Before any evidence on the identity of the bombing suspect was revealed by the FBI, alarmists blamed "Middle Easterners," "Islamic radicals," or "Muslim fundamentalists" and warned that American cities have become a battleground for "Islamic terrorism." In the forty-eight hours following the bombing, almost all media networks became open platforms for these voices.

Criticism of Muslims went beyond the denunciation of Muslim extremists. Muslim symbols, institutions, and religious observances became objects of scorn and agitation. The mere presence of Islamic religious facilities in a particular area was sufficient to infer criminality. This is evident, for example, in the attempt by the *New York Times* to correlate the bombing to the fact that Oklahoma City is home for three mosques. Inflammatory reports prompted an immediate hysterical reaction, which made American Muslims the second victims of the Oklahoma City bombing.

According to the Council on American-Islamic Relations (CAIR), Muslims suffered 222 incidents of harassment and violence, most of which occurred in the first forty-eight hours following the Oklahoma City bombing. Adding to the severity of the offenses, Muslims were pursued by their attackers in the sanctuary of their homes and places of worship (rather than attacked at random during casual encounters). Of course, it would obviously be wrong to ascribe prejudice to American society as a whole. In fact, according to officials with CAIR, anti-Muslim violence comprised isolated incidents believed to have been triggered by sensational media coverage and political scapegoating.

> *"Inflammatory reports prompted an immediate hysterical reaction, which made American Muslims the second victims of the Oklahoma City bombing."*

While alarmists intend to warn Americans against possible threats posed by the Muslim presence in the United States, they seldom discuss who Muslims are and what they do. According to Muslim sources there are 6 million Muslims in the United States. In contrast, American Jews, according to Jewish sources, are 4.1 million strong. Thus, in terms of demography, Islam has replaced Judaism as the largest non-Christian faith in the United States. The history of Islam in America dates as early as the slave trade. It is estimated that about 30 percent of the slaves brought to this country from Africa were Muslim. Once slavery was abolished by Congress in 1870, many African-Americans started searching for their roots. It is estimated that currently about 20 percent of African-Americans profess the Islamic faith.

In addition, a great number of Muslims came to the United States as immigrants. The U.S.-born sons and daughters of these immigrants now form a majority within this category of American Muslims. Contrary to prevailing images, most Muslims living in the country are U.S. citizens and permanent residents; only a negligible percentage comprise foreign students and temporary exiles. To make sense of the Islamic community in America, one has to examine Muslim groups and their activities. Who are these groups? What do they want?

> *"While alarmists intend to warn Americans against possible threats posed by the Muslim presence in the United States, they seldom discuss who Muslims are and what they do."*

A close look at Muslim activism in the United States depicts a community, like other communities in America, that mobilizes its resources to provide for essential services: prayers, schooling, religious and ethnic celebrations and rituals, newspapers, educational materials, conferences, and political expression. American Muslims are building institutions to satisfy their felt need of holding on to their faith. In so doing, Muslims seek to live cooperatively and peacefully with other communities in the United States. Islamic teachings, which are the substance of articulation in Muslim activities, protect children and communities from crime, disease, and other social decay. As such, Muslim activism hardly threatens the security of the United States.

The organized expressions of Islam in America have been intertwined with ethnic affiliation. Primary organizations comprise mosques, Islamic centers, and schools. Every city has at least one mosque or Islamic center. Where Muslims live in large numbers in cities such as Los Angeles and New York, dozens of mosques and Islamic centers are found. Other types of Muslim organizations comprise national constituency groupings and public service institutions.

Mosques, Islamic Centers, and Schools

American Muslims started to build mosques in the early decades of the twentieth century. Albanian Muslim immigrants built a mosque in Maine in 1915 and established another in Connecticut in 1919. Polish-speaking Tatars built a mosque in 1926 in Brooklyn, New York. African-American Muslims established in 1930 the First Muslim Mosque. In 1934 the Lebanese Muslim community opened a mosque in Cedar Rapids, Iowa. The number of mosques increased sharply after the mid-1960s. This period was marked by a sharp increase in Muslim immigration to the United States and by an Islamic religious revival worldwide.

Mosques consist of prayer halls and washing facilities. As Muslim communities grew, Muslims recognized the need to build Islamic centers that featured educational classrooms, libraries, cultural galleries, and youth quarters along with prayer halls and washrooms. In addition, Muslim leaders recognized the need for an organized effort to help local Muslims fulfill religious teachings and rituals in occasions such as marriage, funerals, family disputes, and inheritance rights. By 1990 the number of mosques and Islamic centers reached one thousand. Also, there were ninety-two full-time Islamic schools and seventy others operating on a part-time basis. Full-time schools are accredited by boards of education in their states. They offer religious education in addition to English language, math, and science.

> *"To make sense of the Islamic community in America, one has to examine Muslim groups and their activities."*

The proliferation of Islamic institutions has been brought about at the grassroots level. Islamic centers and schools are operated independently by local Muslim communities. Some of these local centers have grown enough to command national recognition. One such example is the Islamic Center of Southern California. In addition to providing for religious and educational services, it sponsors a magazine, the *Minaret*, and a public affairs office. This center has established dialogue with Christian and Jewish groups in California. Another example of such Islamic centers is *Dar al-Hijrah* (The House of Migration), in Virginia. It has hosted a number of town meetings with elected officials and established working relationships with neighboring churches and local businesses. It also organized a blood drive and collected relief contributions from local Muslims to support the victims of the Oklahoma City bombing.

The ethnic makeup of local Islamic centers depends largely on exogenous factors such as the job and school locations of community members. As a result, most local Muslim communities are ethnically mixed. Islamic centers cooperate on a regional level on matters such as programs to celebrate Muslim holiday seasons, to hold youth camps, or host speakers. Funding for these programs is secured by donations collected following Friday prayers and by regular fund-raising activities. Also, leaders of Islamic centers collect and distribute special almsgivings by local Muslims. About half of the local Islamic centers are affiliated with national groupings.

National Constituency Organizations

As early as 1908 Muslim immigrants started to arrive from the various provinces of the collapsing Ottoman Empire. They were mainly Turks, Kurds, Arabs, and Albanians. The largest wave of immigration from Muslim countries began in the mid-1960s under President Lyndon Johnson, when the government introduced measures relaxing restrictions against immigration from the Middle East and South East Asia.

Immigrant Muslim students established the Muslim Student Association

(MSA) in 1963. Many of these students graduated, found work in the United States, and made America their permanent residence. The MSA has served the U.S.-born sons and daughters of the founders and early members of the organization. One of the main needs that the MSA has fulfilled is the arrangement of Friday prayers on campuses. Currently the MSA comprises a network of 100 chapters in American universities.

Islamic Society of North America (ISNA)

Established in 1982, ISNA has focused on facilitating the development of Islamic centers, mosques, and schools. It has also acted as a coordinating council for a number of Muslim organizations. One of the main organs of ISNA is the North American Islamic Trust (NAIT), which protects the legal ownership of a pool of 250 Islamic centers and 100 Islamic schools. In addition, constituting members of ISNA include the Muslim Arab Youth Association (MAYA), the Muslim Student Association, the Malaysian Islamic Student Group, the Council of Islamic Schools in North America, the Islamic Medical Association, the American Muslim Social Scientists, and the American Muslim Scientists and Engineers. Each of these subgroups has its own members, publications, and meetings.

There are no conditions for individual membership in ISNA except for paying annual dues. ISNA publishes a bimonthly magazine, *Islamic Horizon*, and holds an annual conference attended by thousands of Muslims. Although ISNA is highly mixed, immigrants from Arab origins constitute the largest grouping within its ranks. According to the General Secretary of ISNA, its thirty-third annual conference, which was held in September 1995 in Columbus, Ohio, was

> *"[Islamic centers] organized a blood drive and collected relief contributions from local Muslims to support the victims of the Oklahoma City bombing."*

attended by 12,000 Muslims. About 40 percent of these participants were Arab; the rest came from various ethnic backgrounds.

Islamic Circle of North America (ICNA)

Established in 1974, ICNA focuses on the propagation of Islam. ICNA publishes a monthly magazine, the *Message International*, and holds a national annual conference, which is attended by thousands of participants. ICNA is particularly reputable in the Muslim community for the pamphlets, videotapes, and other literature on Islam it produces and passes out in public places. According to an official with ICNA, the organization receives every day about thirty requests for literature on Islam from prison inmates alone. To satisfy the public desire to know about Islam, ICNA sponsors the toll-free *Dawa* (Propagation) Hotline. In addition, the Sound Vision department has produced videotapes on various aspects of the Islamic faith. It has also developed *al-Qari* (the

Reader), a multimedia program designed to teach any computer user to properly read the Arabic language and recite the Quran.

With headquarters in Queens, New York, ICNA maintains five regional offices. In addition, ICNA's forty chapters are run by individuals from their homes. One feature that distinguishes ICNA from the other groupings is that it accepts only strongly committed Muslims who are willing to volunteer their time for the cause of spreading the message of Islam. ICNA extends its services to all people regardless of ethnic background, although a majority of its members and supporters are descendants of the Indian subcontinent.

Shiite Muslim Groupings

The institutional development of Shiite Muslims in America is not very different from that of their Sunni counterparts, because its principal concern has been the inculcation of Islamic teachings. According to credible Shiite sources, there are about fifty Islamic centers and five full-time schools led by local Shiite communities, particularly in New York, Maryland, Michigan, Illinois, and California. These institutions organize prayers and offer a host of educational and spiritual programs. The religious scholars of about thirty-five mosques established in 1994 the Council of Shiite Muslim Scholars in North America. The council, which acts as a coordinating body of Shiite imams, aspires to facilitate the organization of Muslims in local and national elections, and vows to follow a rapprochement policy with Muslims of other sects.

"The largest wave of immigration from Muslim countries began in the mid-1960s."

Because of linguistic reasons, Shiite organizations are divided across ethnic and language lines. There are Arab and Persian speaking Shiite student groups. These groups have held annual conferences since the early eighties. Such gatherings are attended by thousands of students. Another main group is the Quran Propagation Movement, which is a predominantly Indo-Pakistani group that publishes and distributes the Quran. The Iraqi Islamic Society in Detroit, Michigan, is particularly active among Iraqi Shiites. It combines a religious education agenda and an interest in the political conditions in Iraq. There are African-Americans who adopted Shiite Muslim jurisprudence, but they do not constitute any collective body. Many African-American Muslims do not identify themselves as Shiite or Sunni. However, large organizations such as the ministry of W.D. Muhammad and the National Community are Sunni.

African-American Groups

Fard Muhammad, believed to have been influenced by the Ahmadiyah movement, which originated in the Indian subcontinent, established the Nation of Islam (NOI) in the 1930s. The late Elijah Muhammad became one of Fard's early disciples. When Fard mysteriously disappered in 1934, Elijah took over and made the NOI into an ethnic group, which offered African-American local communities entrepreneurial skills and a sense of self-reliance and self-respect. The NOI built places of worship, schools, and businesses. When Elijah passed away in 1975, his son, W.D. Muhammad, moved the organization into the multi-ethnic, universal concepts of mainstream Islam. Louis Farrakhan, then a disciple of Elijah, insisted on the old teachings of the NOI. When W.D. Muhammad changed the name of the community, Farrakhan claimed the original name for his ministry, which he carries until today.

The Ministry of W.D. Muhammad manages 200 mosques nationwide in addition to other educational institutions and local businesses. Supporters of the new direction led by W.D. Muhammad publish the largest Muslim weekly newspaper: the *Muslim Journal*. According to Ayesha Mustafaa, the newspaper editor, the current circulation of the newspaper has reached 20,000 and continues to grow.

Another mainstream African-American Muslim group is the National Community led by Imam Jamil al-Amin, formerly known as Rap Brown. This community maintains about thirty mosques and focuses on grassroots social activism. African-American Muslim groups are particularly active in countering crime and urban decay. Also, recently they have become active in local politics. In 1992 Charles Bilal of Kountze, Texas, became the first African-American Muslim mayor in U.S. history.

Ethnicity-Based Groupings

Besides the large national bodies, a number of smaller immigrant groupings have been established on the basis of ethnic affinity. Some of these happened to be communities whose members had been adversely affected by events in their countries of origin. The Islamic Association for Palestine (IAP), which was established in 1980 by Palestinian immigrants, is a prime example of this type. IAP activities are felt in Palestinian communities in Chicago, New Jersey, and Dallas.

> *"Muslims seek to live cooperatively and peacefully with other communities in the United States."*

The IAP Information Office publishes the *Muslim World Monitor* in English and *al-Zaytunah* (the *Olive*) in Arabic. In addition, the IAP holds an annual "Jerusalem Festival," which features entertainment performances and fund-raising for relief assistance to refugees in the West Bank and Gaza.

Other such groupings include the Kashmiri American Council which was established in 1991. The council's prime cause is self-determination for Indian occupied Kashmir. The council disseminates information on the situation in Kashmir, particularly on the human rights record in the majority-Muslim State of Kashmir. Also, the council lobbies the U.S. Congress and the American administration on the question of Kashmir. Other American Muslims have recently organized themselves to support the cause of Muslims under oppression in such areas as Bosnia and Chechnya. Groups such as the Balkan Muslim Association and the Congress of Chechen International Organizations are usually led by descendants from these areas of the world.

Public Service Organizations

A number of charities have emerged, especially during the eighties. These include ISNA Indian Muslim Relief, ICNA Relief, the Holy Land Foundation, Islamic Relief, Mercy International, Islamic Relief Organization, Chechnya Relief Fund, Kashmiri Relief Committee, and Somali Relief Committee. The primary focus of these organizations is to provide assistance to refugees and victims of war overseas. They have also offered relief efforts at home. This includes regular contributions to soup kitchens and homeless shelters and assistance to victims of earthquakes, hurricanes, and other disasters, such as the bombing in Oklahoma City. Some Muslim charities are currently working side by side with the Red Cross and Catholic relief groups to help in the U.S.-led effort of rebuilding Bosnia.

The American Muslim Council was established in Washington, DC, in 1990. The council has published a booklet estimating the Muslim population in the United States. It has also sponsored voter registration activities among members of the Muslim community and organized town meetings between elected officials and local Muslim communities. The Washington-based Council on American Islamic Relations (CAIR) challenges media stereotypes on Muslims, provides training material for local activists in public relations, documents anti-Muslim bias and violence, and issues policy research papers and other educational literature. The Muslim Public Affairs Council in Los Angeles has worked to involve Muslims in party politics. Some of its members served as delegates to the Democratic National Convention in 1992.

Muslim Activism Is Not a Threat

The foregoing account of Muslim institution building, which is not representative of all Muslims, shows that the community, like other communities, has added its own ideas and values to the American melting pot. Writings on the "Islamic threat" tend to blur the distinction between the millions of mainstream Muslims and the elements in this community who act violently to press for their perceived grievances. Every community and every cause has its radicals. Educating the public about Muslims and their activities by focusing on fringe elements at the expense of the mainstream will only reinforce stereotypical images, hurt community relations, and create hostilities at odds with the values of tolerance in the pluralistic American society.

Muslim organizations from various backgrounds gathered in a leadership summit in April 1995 to air their concerns over some aspects of the Clinton administration's Omnibus Counterterrorism Act, which was submitted to Congress in February 1995. Muslims believe that the bill may criminalize giving money for peaceful activities, such as running hospitals, to charities led by individuals who sympathize with political opposition groups around the world. Also, Muslims, among others, believe that the proposed act sanctions the formation of special courts to deport legal aliens based on secret evidence. Muslim groups have entered a coalition led by the American Civil Liberties Union opposing the act. However, Muslim groups have supported other aspects of the proposed legislation, such as measures that would facilitate detection of plastic explosives and prohibit the transaction of nuclear materials.

The Unabomber Is Propagating Anti-Industrial Ideas

by Terrorist Group FC (Unabomber)

About the author: *Terrorist Group FC describes itself as an anarchist, anti-industrial group and has claimed responsibility for the series of bombings, starting in May 1978, that the Federal Bureau of Investigation has called the Unabom case.*

I.

Following is the text of the letter received by the New York Times *on Monday, April 24, 1995, from the self-designated "terrorist group FC," claiming responsibility for the serial bombings that the Federal Bureau of Investigation attributes to a single person or group in the case known as Unabom. The document is presented verbatim, with original spelling, emphasis and punctuation.*

[Passage deleted at the request of the F.B.I.]

This is a message from the terrorist group FC.

We blew up Thomas Mosser last December [1994] because he was a Burston-Marsteller executive. Among other misdeeds, Burston-Marsteller helped Exxon clean up its public image after the [1989] Exxon Valdez incident. But we attacked Burston-Marsteller less for its specific misdeeds than on general principles. Burston-Marsteller is about the biggest organization in the public relations field. This means that its business is the development of techniques for manipulating people's attitudes. It was for this more than for its actions in specific cases that we sent a bomb to an executive of this company.

Some news reports have made the misleading statement that we have been attacking universities or scholars. We have nothing against universities or scholars as such. All the university people whom we have attacked have been specialists in technical fields. (We consider certain areas of applied psychology, such as behavior modification, to be technical fields.) We would not want any-

Excerpted from "Text of Letter from 'Terrorist Group,' Which Says It Committed Bombings," *New York Times*, April 26, 1995, and "Excerpts from Manuscript Linked to Suspect in 17-Year Series of Bombings," *New York Times*, August 2, 1995, both texts attributed to Terrorist Group FC.

one to think that we have any desire to hurt professors who study archaeology, history, literature or harmless stuff like that. The people we are out to get are the scientists and engineers, especially in critical fields like computers and genetics. As for the bomb planted in the Business School at the U. of Utah [in October 1981], that was a botched operation. We won't say how or why it was botched because we don't want to give the FBI any clues. No one was hurt by that bomb.

In our previous letter to you we called ourselves anarchists. Since "anarchist" is a vague word that has been applied to a variety of attitudes, further explanation is needed. We call ourselves anarchists because we would like, ideally, to break down all society into very small, completely autonomous units. Regrettably, we don't see any clear road to this goal, so we leave it to the indefinite future. Our more immediate goal, which we think may be attainable at some time during the next several decades, is the destruction of the worldwide industrial system. Through our bombings we hope to promote social instability in industrial society, propagate anti-industrial ideas and give encouragement to those who hate the industrial system.

The FBI has tried to portray these bombings as the work of an isolated nut. We won't waste our time arguing about whether we are nuts, but we certainly are not isolated. For security reasons we won't reveal the number of members of our group, but anyone who will read the anarchist and radical environmentalist journals will see that opposition to the industrial-technological system is widespread and growing.

Why do we announce our goals only now, though we made our first bomb some seventeen years ago [in May 1978]? Our early bombs were too ineffectual to attract much public attention or give encouragement to those who hate the system. We found by experience that gunpowder bombs, if small enough to be carried inconspicuously, were too feeble to do much damage, so we took a couple of years off to do some experimenting. We learned how to make pipe bombs that were powerful enough, and we used these in a couple of successful bombings as well as in some unsuccessful ones.

> *"The people we are out to get are the scientists and engineers, especially in critical fields like computers and genetics."*

[Passage deleted at the request of the F.B.I.]

Since we no longer have to confine the explosive in a pipe, we are now free of limitations on the size and shape of our bombs. We are pretty sure we know how to increase the power of our explosives and reduce the number of batteries needed to set them off. And, as we've just indicated, we think we now have more effective fragmentation material. So we expect to be able to pack deadly bombs into ever smaller, lighter and more harmless looking packages. On the other hand, we believe we will be able to make bombs much bigger than any we've made before. With a briefcase-full or a suitcase-full of explosives we should be able to blow out the walls of substantial buildings.

Clearly we are in a position to do a great deal of damage. And it doesn't appear that the FBI is going to catch us any time soon. The FBI is a joke.

The people who are pushing all this growth and progress garbage deserve to be severely punished. But our goal is less to punish them than to propagate ideas. Anyhow we are getting tired of making bombs. It's no fun having to spend all your evenings and weekends preparing dangerous mixtures, filing trigger mechanisms out of scraps of metal or searching the sierras for a place isolated enough to test a bomb. So we offer a bargain.

> *"Through our bombings we hope to . . . propagate anti-industrial ideas and give encouragement to those who hate the industrial system."*

We have a long article, between 29,000 and 37,000 words, that we want to have published. If you can get it published according to our requirements we will permanently desist from terrorist activities. . . .

How do you know that we will keep our promise to desist from terrorism if our conditions are met? It will be to our advantage to keep our promise. We want to win acceptance for certain ideas. If we break our promise people will lose respect for us and so will be less likely to accept the ideas. . . .

It may be just as well that failure of our early bombs discouraged us from making any public statements at that time. We were very young then and our thinking was crude. Over the years we have given as much attention to the development of our ideas as to the development of bombs, and we now have something serious to say. And we feel that just now the time is ripe for the presentation of anti-industrial ideas. . . .

We encourage you to print this letter.   FC

[Passage deleted at the request of the F.B.I.]

II.

Following are excerpts from a manuscript sent to the New York Times *in June 1995 by the suspect in the Unabom case, a seventeen-year string of bombings. The manuscript, which has been authenticated by the Federal Bureau of Investigation, is titled "Industrial Society and Its Future" and is attributed on its title page to a group called "FC."*

The industrial revolution and its consequences have been a disaster for the human race. They have greatly increased the life expectancy of those of us who live in "advanced" countries, but they have destabilized society, have made life unfulfilling, have subjected human beings to indignities, have led to widespread psychological suffering (in the Third World to physical suffering as well) and have inflicted severe damage on the natural world. The continued development of technology will worsen the situation. It will certainly subject human beings to greater indignities and inflict greater damage on the natural world, it will probably lead to greater social disruption and psychological suffering, and it may lead to increased physical suffering even in "advanced" countries.

The industrial-technological system may survive or it may break down. If it survives, it MAY eventually achieve a low level of physical and psychological suffering, but only after passing through a long and very painful period of adjustment and only at the cost of permanently reducing human beings and many other living organisms to engineered products and mere cogs in the social machine. Furthermore, if the system survives, the consequences will be inevitable: there is no way of reforming or modifying the system so as to prevent it from depriving people of dignity and autonomy.

If the system breaks down, the consequences will still be very painful. But the bigger the system grows the more disastrous the results of its breakdown will be, so if it is to break down it had best break down sooner rather than later.

We therefore advocate a revolution against the industrial system. This revolution may or may not make use of violence; it may be sudden or it may be a relatively gradual process spanning a few decades. We can't predict any of that. But we do outline in a very general way the measures that those who hate the industrial system should take in order to prepare the way for a revolution against that form of society. This is not to be a POLITICAL REVOLUTION. Its object will be to overthrow not governments but the economic and technological basis of the present society. . . .

The Nature of Freedom

We are going to argue that industrial-technological society cannot be reformed in such a way as to prevent it from progressively narrowing the sphere of human freedom. But, because "freedom" is a word that can be interpreted in many ways, we must first make clear what kind of freedom we are concerned with.

By "freedom" we mean the opportunity to go through the power process, with real goals, not the artificial goals of surrogate activities, and without interference, manipulation or supervision from anyone, especially from any large organization. Freedom means being in control (either as an individual or as a member of a SMALL group) of the life-and-death issues of one's existence: food, clothing, shelter and defense against whatever threats there may be in one's environment. Freedom means having power; not the power to control other people but the power to control the circumstances of one's own life. One does not have freedom if anyone else (especially a large organization) has power over one, no matter how benevolently, tolerantly and permissively that power may be exercised. It is important not to confuse freedom with mere permissiveness. . . .

> *"We . . . advocate a revolution against the industrial system. This revolution may or may not make use of violence."*

As for our constitutional rights, consider for example that of freedom of the press. We certainly don't mean to knock that right; it is a very important tool for limiting concentration of political power and for keeping those who do have political power in line by publicly exposing any misbehavior on their part. But freedom of the press is of very little use to the average citizen as an individual. The mass media are mostly under the control of large organizations that are integrated into the system. Anyone who has a little money can have something printed, or can distribute it on the internet or in some such way, but what he has to say will be swamped by the vast volume of material put out by the media, hence it will have no practical effect. To make an impression on society with words is therefore almost impossible for most individuals and small groups. Take us (FC) for example. If we had never done anything violent and had submitted the present writings to a publisher, they probably would not have been accepted. If they had been accepted and published, they probably would not have attracted many readers, because it's more fun to watch the entertainment put out by the media than to read a sober essay. Even if these writings had had many readers, most of those readers would soon have forgotten what they had read as their minds were flooded by the mass of material to which the media expose them. In order to get our message before the public with some chance of making a lasting impression, we've had to kill people. . . .

Technology and the Elite

If the system breaks down there may be a period of chaos, a "time of troubles" such as those that history has recorded at various epochs in the past. It is impossible to predict what would emerge from such a time of troubles, but at any rate the human race would be given a new chance. The greatest danger is that industrial society may begin to reconstitute itself within the first few years after the breakdown. Certainly there will be many people (power-hungry types especially) who will be anxious to get the factories running again.

Therefore two tasks confront those who hate the servitude to which the industrial system is reducing the human race. First, we must work to heighten the social stresses within the system so as to increase the likelihood that it will break down or be weakened sufficiently so that a revolution against it becomes possible. Second, it is necessary to develop and propagate an ideology that opposes technology and the industrial system. Such an ideology can become the basis for a revolution against industrial society if and when the system becomes sufficiently weakened. And such an ideology will help to assure that, if and when industrial society breaks down, its remnants will be smashed beyond repair, so that the system cannot be reconstituted. The factories should be destroyed, technical books burned etc. . . .

The technophiles are taking us all on an utterly reckless ride into the unknown. Many people understand something of what technological progress is doing to us yet take a passive attitude toward it because they think it is inevitable. But we (FC) don't think it is inevitable. We think it can be stopped. . . .

Until the industrial system has been thoroughly wrecked, the destruction of that system must be the revolutionaries' ONLY goal.

The Unabomber Is an Environmentalist Lunatic

by Alan Caruba

About the author: *Alan Caruba is the founder of the National Anxiety Center, a media watchdog group in Maplewood, New Jersey.*

Lost amidst the concern that the Unabomber will strike again if his demands are not met has been the fact that his views and actions reflect the core values of those who, since the 1970s, have been the driving force behind the environmental movement.

The Unabomber's Connection to Radical Environmentalism

The Unabomber's crusade is, in his murderous mind, the logical end result of a movement which holds a deep distrust and contempt for humanity, technology, and what is generally understood to be progress in diverse areas that include agriculture, the science of genetics, medicine, computer technology, and just about everything that contributes to a thriving national and global economy.

In a letter to the *New York Times*, he said, "Through our bombings we hope to promote social instability in industrial society, propagate anti-industrial ideas and give encouragement to those who hate the industrial system. . . . The people who are pushing all this growth and progress garbage deserve to be severely punished."

The man is a lunatic. While it's valuable for everyone to gain some insight to his pathology, publishing his 35,000-word diatribe would not deter him. Al Neuharth, the founder of *USA Today*, has correctly noted that "the manifesto is not news that's fit to print."

To any participant or observer of the environmental movement, it's fairly astonishing that anyone could have failed to notice that views comparable to the Unabomber's have been appearing in print for more than two decades, since the inception of the environmental movement.

In a 1970 book, *Ecotactics*, which had an introduction by Ralph Nader, statements comparable to the Unabomber's can be found on every page. An unidentified writer for a group called ECOS rants against "an aggressive technology and economic system, which, in a rush to provide for and to profit from the human population, destroys other forms of life and contaminates our environment to a degree unprecedented in human history." The writer rejects "a world in which the individual is victimized by the impersonal machinery of his technology." While decrying violence, the writer concludes that "the only natural resource left on this planet that man seems unable to reduce to the disaster level is the capacity for discontent. Our organization, Environment!, is designed to harvest this resource and apply it to the complex problems of survival."

This ECOS writer was right at home with Nader's introductory view that Americans were living in a society of "oppression and suppression" by business and industrial entities. Thus, Nader's first priority was "to deprive the polluters of their unfounded legitimacy." Corporate America, said Nader, is the enemy and, thus, "Top corporate executives crave anonymity. . . ."

The War on Technology

Among the Unabomber's victims have been United Airlines President Percy Wood, in 1980; an advertising executive, Thomas Mosser, in December 1994, and a timber-industry lobbyist, Gilbert Murray, in April 1995. Others have been scientists and computer technologists.

In a *New York Times* article on June 30, 1995, Robert D. McFadden hinted at the contents of the Unabomber's manifesto. It "sketches a nightmarish vision of a deteriorating society and a future in which the human race is at the mercy of intelligent machines created by computer scientists. . . . Out of the chaos, he expressed the hope that a return to 'wild nature' might prevail."

Writing in his book *No Turning Back: Dismantling the Fantasies of Environmental Thinking*, Wallace Kaufman says, "Our progress has been the result largely of Western science and technology. Unlike cultures that have only feared and revered nature, industrialized cultures have pursued dominion over nature and subdued most of its dangerous tendencies, achieving what no other culture has done. No other tradition has developed a sophisticated technology capable of feeding six billion people and monitoring the condition of the environment." While the Unabomber was selecting his victims, Kaufman wrote, "A movement that rejects this tradition is dangerously out of touch with reality. . . ."

> *"Views comparable to the Unabomber's have been appearing in print . . . since the inception of the environmental movement."*

Others Who Share the Unabomber's Beliefs

Who shares the Unabomber's view of industrialized society? Paul Ehrlich, the population doomsayer; Lester Brown, whose Worldwatch Institute has been predicting worldwide environmental disaster for decades; and even our vice president, Albert Gore Jr. In his book, *Earth in the Balance*, Gore says, "The edifice of civilization has become astonishingly complex, but as it grows even more elaborate, we feel increasingly distant from our roots in the earth." Tell that to the millions who visit our many national parks. Currently, the Federal government owns 27 percent of the nation's land mass, much of which is "wild nature."

Disaffected, though dedicated, environmentalists have raised voices of alarm and warning concerning the beliefs that drive the Unabomber. Called "deep ecology," this philosophy fuels groups like Earth First! and fanatical animal rights advocates. In his book, *Green Delusions: An Environmentalist Critique of Radical Environmentalism*, Martin W. Lewis noted that deep ecology is a philosophy best labeled "antihumanist anarchism."

There are several "schools" of deep ecology or environmentalism. They include primitivism, antihumanist anarchism, and eco-Marxism. Lewis notes that "primitivists advocate not merely the return to a small-scale social order proposed by other deep ecologists, but rather the active destruction of civilization."

It's a good description of the Unabomber, but it really doesn't matter what label is attached to him. His presence, his actions, and his insanity represent the ultimate goals of the core values shared by those who seek to direct the environmental movement, both nationally and globally.

The history of the environmental movement in the U.S. has been to impose a huge matrix of laws designed, not just to set reasonable standards for the environment, but which have had the result of impeding whole sectors of the economy. Environmental laws currently represent 30 percent of Washington's entire regulatory budget.

Our Republic of Technology

The good news is that the Unabomber, whether he is captured at last or not, is on the wrong side of history. In 1978, the Pulitzer prize–winning historian, Daniel Boorstin, wrote a book, *The Republic of Technology*. "Our Republic of Technology is not only more democratic, but also more in the American mode. Anyone can be a citizen. Largely a creation of American civilization in the last century, this republic offers a foretaste of American life in our next century. It is open to all,

> *"[The Unabomber's] philosophy fuels groups like Earth First! and fanatical animal rights advocates."*

because it is a community of shared experience." Anyone who has logged onto the World Wide Web of the Internet already knows that.

Those who have died or been maimed by the Unabomber have been the victims of the growing desperation of hard core environmentalism and ecological fanaticism. They have been the foot soldiers of a new age of technology, ushering in worldwide democracy that will create a civilization whose benefits spread throughout the globe. You cannot un-invent anything, nor can you bomb it out of existence.

Chapter 3

Do the Media Encourage Terrorism?

CURRENT CONTROVERSIES

Chapter Preface

When the Alfred C. Murrah Federal Building was bombed on April 19, 1995, journalists scrambled to report whatever information they could find. It wasn't until reporters shifted their attention to the search for the perpetrator that the American public voiced its displeasure with their efforts. Initial news reports quoted terrorist experts who speculated that the attack was perpetrated by Arab terrorists. Upon the arrest of former soldier Timothy McVeigh, coverage zeroed in on conservative paramilitary groups.

According to some, the media's mention of the Middle East as the source of the attacker was premature and xenophobic, prompted by an unhealthy reluctance to look within and examine America's domestic threats. "The ethnocentrism of the news media was clear in two ways," argues Howard J. Ehrlich of the Prejudice Institute. "First, in the stereotyping of Arabs and other Middle Easterners; and second, in the denial that ordinary Americans could engage in terrorist activities." Referring to the FBI's initial identification of its chief suspects as John Doe Numbers 1 and 2, *Newsweek*'s Jonathan Alter wrote, "'John Doe' is not an Arab name." Alter argued that the "huge bomb blew up some huge stereotypes" and forced people to reevaluate their preconceptions about others. "That self-described 'patriot' who looks like John Wayne could be a baby-killer," he warned.

Others found the media's subsequent focus on militias unfair and neglectful of important links to Middle Eastern terrorist groups. Writer William F. Jasper, for one, argues that by directing attention towards right-wing antigovernment groups the media obediently furthered the Clinton administration's efforts to associate Republicans and "everyone to the starboard of Hillary Clinton" with the bombing. Instead, he contends, newspeople should have investigated federal agents' failure to pursue viable leads about Middle Eastern accomplices to McVeigh. "If you're looking for real breakthroughs on this critically important case," he writes in the *New American*, "you're sure not going to get them from CBS, PBS, CNN, ABC, NBC, the *Washington Post*, the *New York Times*, or any of their sycophantic imitators."

As global communications technologies continue to evolve, concern grows over how the media should respond to terrorism and what role they should play. The extent to which media and terrorism influence one another is debated throughout the following chapter.

Terrorists Rely on Media Coverage

by Terry Anderson

About the author: *Terry Anderson is a journalist and former chief Middle East correspondent for the Associated Press (AP). In 1985 he was taken hostage by terrorists in Lebanon and held in captivity for nearly seven years. In 1992 and 1993 he served as a fellow at the Freedom Forum Media Studies Center at Columbia University in New York City.*

When Israel invaded south Lebanon on 6 June 1982, I had been covering southern Africa out of Johannesburg for nearly a year and was eager to get out. Southern Africa was quiet and I was restless. Lebanon was a war—the world's biggest story—and I was a journalist. The Middle East was the natural place to go.

Lebanon was exciting. The country fascinated me with its religious diversity, its endless complications, its small feuds and larger wars. The Maronites, the Sunnis, the Shi'a, the Druze, the Palestinians—each had splintered factions and shifting goals. There was incredible violence at a scale and intensity I had never seen before in my six years as a foreign correspondent. But there were also the stubborn, brave, independent people who somehow survived the brutality.

By 1982, Western reporters had become accustomed to wandering freely around Lebanon—subject to the occasional verbal abuse or roughing up—but accepted by even the most radical of factions as journalists, independent of and apart from the U.S. and British governments. A year later, however, the atmosphere had begun to change.

Left in Chains

Beginning with the victory of Ayatollah Khomeini in Iran, Iranian money poured into Lebanon to influence the Shi'a, a Muslim sect disaffected with their native leadership. Religious conflicts intensified, and Washington's shifted position on Lebanon inspired a more personal hatred for the United States in particular, and the West in general. In Beirut, more and more bearded men—young Shi'a—appeared on the streets, carrying signs echoing Iran's revolutionary fer-

Terry Anderson, "Terrorism and Censorship: The Media in Chains," *Journal of International Affairs,* Summer 1993, vol. 47, no. 1 (endnotes have been omitted); © 1993 The Trustees of Columbia University in the City of New York. Reprinted with permission.

vor and anti-Western propaganda. Journalists' encounters with such bitter gun-men became a little harder to escape without injury.

In December 1983, a group of Iranian-inspired Shi'a launched an attempt to destabilize Kuwait with attacks on the U.S. and French embassies, power sta-tions and other installations. Despite the destruction, the attempt failed miser-ably. Hundreds of Shi'a were rounded up, and 17 were charged. Some were given long prison terms and others were handed death sentences. As it took place far off in the Gulf, the event was soon forgotten—at least by the West. There was no immediate connection with events in Lebanon, no hint that the repercussions would involve half a dozen countries and leave Westerners, in-cluding me, in chains for months or years.

By the time I was kidnapped in March 1985, the U.S. embassy and the Ma-rine barracks had been bombed; Malcolm Kerr, the president of the American University, Beirut had been murdered; and a handful of Westerners had been taken hostage. Beirut had turned into a kind of perpetual chaos.

The U.S. embassy had been quietly warning Americans to leave Beirut—a warning that most news people just ignored, although a few took the advice or moved to East Beirut, which was considered a much safer place. I stayed, deter-mined to cover the story. On 16 March 1985, I was kidnapped.

The Islamic Jihad [a political Islamic group] claimed responsibility and de-manded the release of the Da'wa 17, the 17 jailed in Kuwait. Thus began my al-most seven years in captivity—seven years during which I witnessed firsthand the tenuous and powerful relationship between terrorism and the press.

The Media-Terrorism Relationship

There can be no denying it: The media are part of the deadly game of terror-ism. Indeed, the game can scarcely be played without them. In my experience, publicity has been at once a primary goal and a weapon of those who use terror against innocent people to advance political causes or to simply cause chaos. And they are quite good at the public relations game—which is why their at-tacks, kidnappings and murder are usually so spectacularly vicious.

In my opinion, the very reporting of a political kidnapping, an assassination or a deadly bombing is a first victory for the terrorist. Without the world's attention, these acts of viciousness are pointless. Furthermore, unless the terrorist can attach his political mes-sage to the headlines he has caused, he has failed. When newspapers run

> *"Publicity has been at once a primary goal and a weapon of those who use terror against innocent people."*

long analyses about the Islamic Jihad, its hatred of Israel and the West and its reliance on fundamentalist interpretations of Islam, "Islamic Jihad" becomes a legitimate force—something politicians and civilians alike must take seriously.

No matter that the analyses may be uniformly condemnatory, and that the reader has automatically and completely rejected the organization's premises.

The acts that have won terrorists this public notice—whether kidnapping or bombing or murder—are seen by terrorists as successful. They have forced the world to take notice of them, indicating their sense of self-importance.

The Role of the Media

Everyone uses the media. Journalists are accustomed to being used by presidents, kings, parliaments, entertainers, political activists or ordinary citizens trying to attract the world's attention—that's a major part of the media's role. The media carry messages to anyone from anyone with the knowledge, skill or importance to make use of them. It may be propaganda or it may be truth, but either way, the media carry powerful influence.

I was raised in journalism by old-fashioned editors who ingrained in me a fundamental belief in objectivity. According to my teachers, journalists were meant to present the facts and the facts only, and the audience—armed with seemingly unbiased material—was appointed to analyze and draw conclusions. The journalistic ideal means by allowing the public access to the widest possible range of information, they will be able to judge that which rings true and seems useful, and then utilize it to develop informed opinions and make wise decisions. The ideal is tested constantly in this age of mass marketing, public relations and so-called spin doctors who attempt to distribute information with a specific goal in mind.

> *"It may be propaganda or it may be truth, but either way, the media carry powerful influence."*

But there are facts and there is truth. During my years in captivity, I had plenty of time to reassess the journalist's role in covering news. Objectivity and neutrality are vital, but they do not necessarily entail putting aside a personal desire to see the violence that we cover come to an end.

Terrorist Manipulation of the Media

I am not the first to question the precarious relationship between media and terrorism. A wide-ranging debate about the subject was initiated after the seizure of the U.S. embassy and the taking of American hostages in Iran in 1979. The Teheran hostage crisis dominated network television coverage of Iran—indeed, the percentage of stories about that country escalated from about 1 percent in the early 1970s to over 30 percent by 1980.

A half decade later, one event in particular made clear the symbiotic relationship between the media and terrorism, setting off a second flurry of analysis: the hijacking of TWA Flight 847 to Beirut. Here, the media—television in particular—became the primary conduit between the terrorists and the governments.

During the hijacking, the captors set up televised interviews with the hostages and held the first televised hostage news conference. Early on, the event turned into a shameful circus with one television network buying the rights to the story from the Shi'a Amal militia, and thereafter taking over the Summerland Hotel where the hostages were trotted out to meet the press. The amount of money involved is unknown except to those who paid and received it, but rumors suggested it was in the tens to hundreds of thousands of dollars, cash. Regrettably, the fact that one American, Navy diver Robert Stethem, had already been murdered by the hijackers and dozens of lives were in the balance became only a reason for more hype—not for caution and prudence. This was a big story; it was especially a television story and the media were not about to turn off their cameras.

Sending Signals

In my situation, the Islamic Jihad did not wage a similar all-out public relations campaign. For months on end, they offered the media so little information that we hostages were deemed forgotten, and friends, relatives and colleagues felt compelled to wage their own campaign for publicity. But when the Islamic Jihad did use tactics to manipulate the media, they were generally successful.

The players on both sides of this long game displayed their understanding of the media in many ways. The Reagan administration first tried to cut the press out of the game. They insisted that there would be no "deals with terrorists," while pursuing the favorite tactic of diplomats—secret negotiations. When the so-called arms-for-hostages deal blew up in their faces [the Reagan administration secretly agreed to trade arms to Iran for release of the hostages, violating the U.S. weapons embargo against Iran and other countries believed linked to terrorist groups], they tried to use the press, through purported unofficial leaks in a campaign to "devalue" the terrorists.

When that failed as well, they sent signals to Iran, which sponsors and funds Hizballah [a Shi'ite Muslim fundamentalist group in Lebanon whose name means Party of God and whose members claim allegiance to Iran], that they were willing, even eager to discuss the matter. Iran returned the signals frequently. Yet it was in comments to independent newspapers, or by government-controlled newspapers in Iran, that the idea of a swap of hostages for Lebanese prisoners held by Israel was first publicly suggested. The kidnappers blatantly used the press to push their agenda, fi-

> *"Many terrorist organizations have press offices, complete with spokesmen, press releases and audiovisual material."*

nally signalling their willingness to talk, and even to publicize their disagreements with Iranian sponsors.

Similar manipulation of the media was shown by captors of American officials at the U.S. embassy in Iran five years earlier. Hostage-takers aired their demands through staged demonstrations scheduled to coincide with nightly newscasts and ABC's "America Held Hostage" program, now known as "Nightline." Many terrorist organizations have press offices, complete with spokesmen, press releases and audiovisual material.

The Only Connection

In our case, photographs and videos were released along with demands as if our faces—mine in particular—were some sort of instantaneous press pass. No media outlet could deny their audience, and especially not a hostage's relatives, a glimpse of the Americans held in Lebanon. It was a natural way to grab the world's attention.

Still, the videos—a clear manipulation of the media by our captors—were also our only connection to our families, and for that reason alone, allowed us a bit of hope. At least the world would know we were alive. It was by no means an easy thing to do. When one day one of my keepers told me to make a video-tape, I thought long and hard about whether I should refuse. I reflected on my Marine Corps training about how to behave as a prisoner, and struggled with the notion of aiding and comforting the enemy.

> *"Terrorists pay enormous attention to the news reports about the things they do."*

But in the end, I decided nobody would believe any of it; nobody would really think these were my opinions, and it was likely to be the only way I could reassure my family that I was alive and well. So I read their propaganda—rationalizations of their actions, attacks on President Reagan, vague but ominous threats couched in harsh language—and by so doing, I played a part in the media game.

There were times, however, when the media game—especially the release of videos—backfired on our captors. Terrorists pay enormous attention to the news reports about the things they do. In 1986, when Father Martin Jenco was released, he carried with him a videotape made by fellow hostage David Jacobsen. In the tape, Jacobsen sent his condolences to the "wife and children" of William Buckley, who had died some time before in prison. Jacobsen did not know that Buckley was not married.

An over-enthusiastic journalist used that discrepancy to construct a theory that there was a so-called secret message on that tape. Worse, his television network prominently speculated on the theory. We were allowed by our captors to watch the first few television news reports of our companion's release. I remember seeing a yellow banner across the television screen in one report, emblazoned "Secret Message?" The question mark, I guess, was meant to justify use of the story.

Our captors also saw the story. They were very paranoid people, and believed it. They were extremely angry. We suffered, losing the few privileges we had—books, pen, paper—and were dumped in a vile and filthy underground prison for the next six months. We were lucky one or more of us was not killed.

The Question of Censorship

How do we balance the public's right to know—so vital to our society—and the duty of the press to reveal, with the knowledge that publicity seems so often to serve the purposes of terrorists? Because terrorists want and need publicity, should we therefore *not* give it to them? Should there be censorship, imposed or voluntary, about such news reports?

Persistent analyses of how the media should and should not respond to terrorism will continue as long as such activities take place, and we may never come up with satisfactory answers. I believe—like all journalists I know—that the press must fulfill its duty to expose and present information objectively, thereby serving the public good. Censorship by government officials would be a grievous mistake, and so-called general guidelines are too often vague or unsuited to particular events to be useful in these kinds of situations.

However, when lives are at stake, journalistic self-restraint may be necessary. In some cases, it will be imperative that information be reported even if the result is loss of life. In others, a journalist will have to choose whether to release, delay or withhold information. In each case, the individual journalist must ask him or herself: Should I report this if it jeopardizes a human life?

When the arms-for-hostages deal was revealed in the press, I was due to be the next hostage released. New clothes to wear home had been bought for me. But the news reports blew the whole deal out of the water. It was five years before I would finally be free. Nonetheless, I agree with the decision my colleagues in the press made to make the negotiations public. The very highest officials in the land, even the president, were engaged in talks that directly contradicted their public statements, indeed broke both U.S. law and violated the Constitution. That was more important than my fate, or that of the others still held.

When to Withhold

Such is not often the case. There are times, I have learned, when information *should* be withheld. In early 1983, when I was reporting on the Middle East out of Beirut, I became aware through impeccable sources that the Palestine Liberation Organization was negotiating with the kidnappers of David Dodge, another president of the American University, Beirut who had been snatched in 1982. The PLO believed it had some hope of winning Dodge's freedom, and at the very least had confirmed he was alive and well—something no one had been able to do in the six months since his abduction.

Though I had second thoughts about the wisdom of reporting the negotiations, I allowed my boss to talk me into filing the story. It got "good play"—headlines in many papers in the United States. My sources, who had not realized how much they were telling me, were furious, and fearful that reports would kill the negotiations. As it happens, they did not: Dodge was eventually released. Still, I knew I had made a mistake. The story served no purpose and advanced no ideal, except maybe my career. If I

> *"How do we balance the public's right to know—so vital to our society— . . . with the knowledge that publicity seems so often to serve the purposes of terrorists?"*

had wanted Dodge's family to know I had learned he was alive and well, I could have told them privately. As it was, my report could very well have blown the secret talks away, as publicity later did to the arms-for-hostages deal. It could have cost the elderly Dodge more years in filthy prisons.

That realization had a strong effect on me. When I later had occasion to learn information about people who had been kidnapped, I was very, very careful how I used it, and often did not.

There is no simple formula. My experience as both journalist and hostage has provided me with a personal look at terrorists' manipulation of the media and the impact of the media's coverage of such events. The reply seems obvious: Don't give the terrorists what they want. Don't give them publicity. Don't report on their demands, or even—for the most adamant of media critics—on their actions. If they cannot expect publicity, they will go away.

No Simple Formula

As with most obvious answers, this one is both philosophically mistaken and practically impossible. We are, after all, a democracy. That means at least theoretically—and I believe in practice to a greater extent than cynics would have us believe—that the public decides important issues by electing its representatives and changing them when they do poorly. They cannot do so intelligently without a free press, for any controls on the press rapidly become political ones, and in my opinion, will be used by those in power to keep themselves there.

> *"Any controls on the press rapidly become political ones, and . . . will be used by those in power to keep themselves there."*

But even if the theory behind full reporting of terrorist acts is sound, what about the practice? Surely the media behave irresponsibly often in the single-minded pursuit of headlines or air time.

We are a nation that has learned to be very suspicious of our leaders, and in particular any attempt by them to overtly control the information to which we have access. A bomb in a public place, or even the kidnapping of a prominent person, are not events that can be easily hidden or ignored. Trying to do so simply gives rise to rumors and false reports—always exaggerating the extent of the incident, and therefore giving the terrorist something he likes even more than publicity—the spreading of fear. I have found that the best antidote to fear is information, even if the information is bad.

Furthermore, the media are not a single entity that can be cautioned, leaned on or controlled. It is difficult to get a group of journalists to agree on something as simple as a basic code of ethics. It is unrealistic to expect any widespread voluntary restraint in matters that involve such attention-grabbing events as terrorist attacks.

Another factor that mitigates against control is that the public does not want it. Despite disparagement of the media for its so-called sensationalism, people seem to want blood-and-guts reports in their daily newsfare. A news organization that does not supply this kind of variety will not last long.

Accepting Responsibility

The philosophical justification for full reporting on terrorist acts does not give journalists a free hand. In each case they must weigh the theoretical or philosophical value of what they do with the fact that individual human lives are at stake. What they report can have a direct impact on the victims, as terrorists pay enormous attention to the news reports about the things they do.

I tell my colleagues: In each and every report you do where a human life is at risk, you must see in your mind that person's face. You must understand that what you report might well kill the person, and accept the responsibility for that. That doesn't mean you will abandon or even tone down your report. In some cases, one person's life, or even the lives of several people, cannot outweigh the necessity to publish the story.

When a government pleads with journalists to withhold stories about terrorists or terrorist incidents because of national security, or danger to negotiations involving hostages, should the journalist bow to those entreaties? Should the well-being of the hostages override all other considerations, as far as journalists are concerned? Or are there other things that are more important? I believe that each of these questions that so many journalists encounter in their work can only be answered individually, and as each case occurs. They should be, and I believe for the most part are, answered with intelligence and responsibility, and a full and careful regard for the lives that may be at stake. But general "guidelines" too often do not fit all cases. Certainly, we should not allow or implicitly approve censorship by government officials, who will try to impose censorship in any case. Public approval of their acts simply encourages an even heavier hand.

> *"In some cases, one person's life, or even the lives of several people, cannot outweigh the necessity to publish the story."*

The Media Further the Goals of Terrorists

by A.P. Schmid

About the author: *A.P. Schmid is a historian and associate professor of international relations at the University of Leiden in the Netherlands. He serves as the university's senior research fellow at the Center for the Study of Social Conflicts and is research director for the Interdisciplinary Research Project on Root Causes of Human Rights Violations.*

Many observers see what Eugene H. Methvin calls a "symbiotic relationship" between insurgent terrorists and Western news media. Western media have been blamed for being "accomplices" to terrorism. Television, in particular, has been singled out for criticism. Richard Clutterbuck called it the most powerful weapon in the terrorist's arsenal. Margaret Thatcher said that we "must find a way to starve the terrorists and hijackers of the oxygen of publicity on which they depend." In the United Kingdom, there has been a suggestion for the establishment of an Institute for the Mass Media whose ethical code would be binding for all editors of major media. Irresponsible or anti-social use of the power of the mass media could, in this view, be punished by a withdrawal of the license of a journalist or station editor. Government censorship in reaction to terrorist and guerrilla campaigns is frequent in Third World nations. At the same time, censorship is one of the preconditions for state terrorism which depends on secrecy as much as insurgent terrorism appears to depend on publicity. . . .

Case Study: The TWA #847 Incident

Let us focus on one incident and look at the way one American television network (NBC) covered it. Research, incidentally has found no significant difference in coverage between the three major U.S. networks. Similarity in organization and production formats seem to account for this homogeneity of ABC, CBS and NBC.

The incident analysed is a dual-phase incident, that is, not a brief shooting or bombing incident, but one which consists of a phase of initial violence or threat

Excerpted from A.P. Schmid, "Terrorism and the Media: The Ethics of Publicity," *Terrorism and Political Violence,* vol. 1, no. 4 (October 1989). Reprinted by permission of the Carnegie Council on Ethics and International Affairs, New York City.

of violence and an outcome which is left undetermined at the moment of initiation. Dual-phase incidents (the term was coined by Martha Crenshaw) consist mainly of occupations, acts of kidnapping and hostage-taking. Since the fate of some victims is left in suspense and a considerable period of time passes between beginning and end, such incidents have the format of an open-ended drama, a format comparable to a fictional television series. The incident we want to look at is the hijacking of a Trans World Airlines jet (Flight 847 from Cairo to Rome) on 14 June 1985. The incident began shortly after the aircraft left Athens airport and involved initially 153 hostages (including the crew). The hijackers from Islamic Jihad, a Shi'ite Muslim group, demanded the release of 776 Shi'ites, held in Israel. The aircraft was ordered to fly to Beirut by the two hijackers and proceeded from there to Algiers and back, releasing at each stop a number of passengers, mainly women and children. One American military man, Robert D. Stethem, was killed, and the possibility that the remaining 39 American hostages would also be "finished off"—as the hijackers put it—dominated the following 16 days, before the negotiations led to a deal after the Amal leader, Nabih Berri, had taken over the hostages and became the spokesman of the Shi'ite terrorists. The incident generated a tremendous amount of publicity.

Televised Coverage

With regard to the coverage by NBC, the following picture emerges from a content analysis conducted by Tony Atwater:

During the 17-day period of the TWA 847 incident NBC's "Nightly News" devoted an average of nine stories each day to the crisis, altogether almost four full hours. This was two-thirds of the total newstime during that period or, in relation to the number of other stories, a full 61 percent of all stories were incident-related; 68 percent of the stories on the crisis were reporter stories; 29 percent of the TWA stories were anchor stories; and only 2.5 percent were commentaries (a total of four commentaries were given by John Chancellor). If we look at the sources of the stories containing interviews we find that U.S. citizens (presumably hostage-linked) were the main source (44 percent), public officials the second largest (38 percent), technical experts were interviewed in 8 percent of the 99 interviews and interest group leaders—presumably also sources sympathetic to terrorists among them—in 9 percent of the cases. This picture is reflected in the topics of the stories.

> *"Such incidents [as kidnapping and hostage-taking] have the format of an open-ended drama, a format comparable to a fictional television series."*

The result of this content analysis indicates, rather surprisingly, that the terrorists and their accomplices received less than 5 percent of the stories. Less surprisingly, this content analysis reveals that little background and context is given to increase public understanding. The U.S. government and its Israeli ally receive most attention, almost ten times as much as the "terrorist" side. Almost equal attention goes to the hostages. By receiving such an amount of exposure, they invited widespread identification. Ben Bradlee of the *Washington Post* put it tersely, "As soon as the hostages appeared on television, they were safe." The exposure increased the price of the 39 U.S. hostages and made their potential sacrifice extremely costly for the American and Israeli governments. As we know, the Israelis released 756 imprisoned Shi'ites in the aftermath of the incident, presumably as a consequence of a negotiated deal. . . .

Media Power

What is the power of the media? Every day they are able to make a selection of an occurrence from the lives of five billion people, and give it a prominence in the perception of hundreds of millions of people, which alters their attitudes and behaviour in ways that are difficult to predict or control. In a sense, it is power without responsibility for the consequences. If power, as defined by Dennis Wrong, is "the capacity of some persons to produce intended and foreseen effects on others," the power of the media is then, to some extent, a blind one. How do editors exercise this power? The criterion they exercise in their daily division of the world into a huge dark zone and tiny areas of bright spotlights is based on the quality of "news value." Journalists pretend to have a nose for news that other people do not have. The question, "What is news?" is answered by references to the "secret ability of the newsmen," and to their "innate judgement." Newsworthiness is established by journalists and accepted by the audience who seeks news.

> *"What the terrorists have discovered is that, by producing bad news, they can gain newsworthiness and attention."*

Over time, a certain consensus as to what news is important has evolved. Galtung and Ruge have pointed out that Western news values favour events that are about elite persons, elite nations and negative happenings. Bad news sells well because it plays on the fears of the audience. What the terrorists have discovered is that, by producing bad news, they can gain newsworthiness and attention. Their violence raises them, if the media pick up the staged event, from anonymity and gives them identity. There are several elements that establish newsworthiness, and the more of these a terrorist actor manages to expose in an act of violence, the more likely he is to create a media event. I asked a number of editors why terrorism is newsworthy. Their answers revealed three clusters of elements:

(1) It was pointed out that acts of terrorism "arouse public alarm" because of their "sheer ruthlessness," their "cruel and indiscriminate use of violence" and their "unpredictability" that "affronts basic values."

(2) The editors stressed the fact that acts of terrorism are often "dramatic and theatrically exciting," that "readers readily identify with the victims," and that the "drama [was] rooted in the fact that it could happen to each of us."

95

(3) The third cluster of answers centered around the fact that "terrorism creates political crisis," "signals dissension," "exposes security lapses" and has "political and social repercussions" and "undermines either democracy or dictatorships."

The TWA Hostage Crisis of 1985

The TWA hostage crisis contained a great number of these elements to make it newsworthy for American and Western audiences. The two hijackers did not explicitly demand publicity. The choice to give the episode the extraordinary publicity was essentially a choice of the media themselves. They decided that the hijacking of an American Boeing 727, with dozens of Americans aboard, was "news." As the story developed and caught the imagination of the American public, the American president was beginning to feel political pressure build up. After 72 hours, President Reagan was forced to rush back from Camp David and call and announce a National Security Council meeting. With public attention growing he could not afford to appear indifferent or inactive. There were probably thousands of the 237 million Americans at that moment in various forms of distress at home and abroad, but the media's focus on 39 hijacked Americans turned this episode into a national security issue. In other words, the media had managed to set the agenda for the President of the United States and for American public opinion for the next two weeks.

The media were not just neutral observers but simply one of the four principal actors in a co-production. Each principal actor was in a different "business": the terrorists in the blackmail business, the hostages in the survival business, the media in the human interest business, and the American president in the national security business. For two weeks they would interact with the media being the main link between them. While they did not all have equal power, the television tube somehow gave them equal roles in the real-life drama. An anchorman could link them to each other in front of the American public and compel them to interact. Dan Rather, for instance, asked one hostage in the CBS News Special Report: ". . . do you have any particular message for President Reagan and the other decision-makers in this country?"

"The media's profuse exposure of the hostage families and their grief . . . played into the hands of the terrorists."

This is no longer reporting what happens but becoming a facilitating participant. The hostage, naturally enough, was glad to be asked, and reminded Ronald Reagan of what Abraham Lincoln had said, that the American "government [was] for and by the people of the country, and not special interests outside of our nation."

This was an appeal in front of the American public to put the lives of individual Americans above the specific interest Israel had in the situation and thereby placed some pressure on the American president. The ultimate result was the exchange of 39 Americans against some 750 prisoners in Israel. How this result was arrived at is difficult to reconstruct without access to the archives. However, it is not unreasonable to assume that the following mechanism stood central:

The media, as Jack Smith, vice president of CBS News, admitted, "manufactured a state of mind, a desire for more information, in the minds of the American public." The American public identified with the American hostages, and the price to sacrifice them to the policies of the Reagan administration, let alone the policies of Israel, became very high. Dying for America was one thing, dying for the muddled Middle East policy of the Reagan administration or the interests of an expansionist Israel another. The exposure of the hostages and their families had an effect that Tom Lentos, member of the Senate Committee on Foreign Affairs, characterized with these words:

> *"The media's coverage had not only provided information but had served as a channel for intimidation."*

> . . . focusing on individual tragedies, interviewing the families of people in anguish, in horror, in nightmare, completely debilitates national policymakers from making rational decisions in the national interest . . . [w]hat is most shocking is . . . that the public opinion polls indicated that a very large proportion of the American people were ready to yield to terrorists. . . . There is no way to conduct foreign policy for 237 million people by focusing on the tragedy of an individual whose husband or wife or child is a hostage.

A Greater Stake

What one could call "the terrorist side" received only 4.4 percent of the total number of stories on NBC. This probably had more to do with the fact that the terrorists were not available for interviews than with the fact that the media did not see fit to talk with them. The result of the shortage of terrorist footage was that the media turned to the families of the hostages when there was a lull of information in order to keep the story alive and going. The families of the hostages were only too eager to talk to the media. The U.S. government had actively discouraged family members of individuals kidnapped in Lebanon from seeking contacts with the media, suggesting that it would hurt what U.S. congressional documents referred to as "quiet diplomacy." Yet quiet diplomacy brought little or no results while megapublicity brought pressure on the American government to bring the hostages in the limelight back at almost any price.

As Jack Smith, CBS vice president, put it: "I think that the negotiators had a greater stake in seeking that they were released once that they had been shown that way." And he also claimed credit for the ultimate result: "We believe that our coverage played a constructive role in ensuring the well-being of the hostages and perhaps in facilitating their release."

For the hostage families, media attention was a kind of "insurance policy" (as ABC's vice president for news practices, Robert Siegenthaler, put it) that the government would not sacrifice Americans to the national interest. They did not, on the whole, feel used by the media, but wanted to use them as much as they could. Their interests and those of the terrorists were identical; they both wanted the American government to give in and put pressure on Israel to negotiate a deal that would lead to the release of the hostages.

The media's profuse exposure of the hostage families and their grief thereby played into the hands of the terrorists. The outcome—successful for the hostages and the terrorists—undermined the American administration's declaratory policy of "No bargaining, no concessions" and probably increased the likelihood of imitation by other terrorists. In the words of Fred W. Friendly of the Columbia Graduate School of Journalism: "Tragically, the final result of the imperfections of the coverage of Flight 847 is that television probably inadvertently advanced the cause of terrorism—encouraging another hijacking, while at the same time paradoxically saving the 39 hostages." Yet, we may ask, was it just a question of the "imperfections of the coverage"? Is not something structurally wrong with this kind of media coverage?

Commercial Competitive Pressure

The main reason why the coverage was so intense was the competition between the major networks. The search for scoops is something that is rewarding for the individual journalist in terms of status and professional awards. On the institutional level the gain is a higher market share and, consequently, higher returns from advertisements. William Henry of *Time* magazine noted that the networks shamelessly bragged about how the crisis hyped their ratings. All three networks registered increased audiences as the story went into its second week. CBS Evening News counted almost one million extra television households. Earlier hostage episodes have produced similar rating increases. The Tehran hostage crisis of 1979 produced in the first 42 days of the 444-day happening an 18 percent increase in ratings for ABC, CBS and NBC. Each percentage point of increase ratings meant in 1979, on an annual basis, a revenue increase of $30 million.

> *"A vicious circle is set in motion into which terrorists inject again and again their electrifying newsworthy attacks."*

The production of audiences that can be sold to advertisers requires repeated gripping action footage which is often not there in long episodes of hostage situations. To keep interest in a rewarding story alive, media can interview, as critic J. Powell put it sarcastically, "the second cousin of the man who used to date the wife of a hostage." The cheapest way of keeping the story alive was Walter Cronkite's daily count: "And that's the way it is in this, the 185th day of captivity for the Americans in Tehran."

The psychological effect of this count up and other prolongation techniques was devastating for the Carter administration. Fifty out of more than 230 million Americans were held hostage, but "America [was] Held Hostage"; in the rhetoric of the media, "America was Under the Gun." The mood created by this constant harping on the same theme helped to bring about the Reagan backlash. The commercialism of American television thereby helped to elevate, fittingly, a former media celebrity to the highest office of the United States.

How Much Coverage Is Enough?

The TWA hostage crisis was an example of saturation coverage. But how much coverage is enough? And: what is too much? There is no absolute answer; only a relative one is possible. Again I have to fall back on the Tehran embassy incident for figures. In the first year of the Iran story, CBS devoted 1,026 minutes to the 50 hostages. Compare this to the amount of time spent on stories of Vietnam in 1972, when there were initially still more than 150,000 U.S. troops there. CBS spent almost the same amount of time (1,092 minutes) on Vietnam. In other words, 50 U.S. hostages in Iran received 3,000 times more coverage than 50 G.I.s in Vietnam. Admittedly, this is a questionable way of comparing things, but it makes clear that the event and the amount of coverage stand in no reasonable relationship to each other.

> *"Terrorists use the media and the media use terrorism."*

There is another way of comparison on a quantitative level: during the TWA incident, CBS spent 62 percent of its total evening news time on this story, NBC was one percentage point higher while ABC devoted 68 percent of its Nightly News to this story alone. In other words, for more than two weeks, this single story was almost twice as important for the media as all the other events happening in the world together. Surely, this loss of any sense of proportion by these commercial networks makes one wonder whether they are fit to determine the news value of events.

News Value

I think that a fruitful discussion on the nexus terrorism-media should focus on the principles linked to the assignment of "news value." It has been said that war is too dangerous to be left to the generals. The assessment of news value, too, should not be the sole prerogative of those network generals who decide every day what hundreds of millions of people will see that night on the picture tube. The power of the media carries great responsibility regarding its use. To whom should the media be responsible? To the government? The government is usually a party to the conflict and therefore ill-suited as an arbiter. Should the reporters and editors be responsible to the consumer, the public? . . .

One effect of the TWA hostage crisis was that it generated fear among American citizens to travel to Europe and some Mediterranean countries. The media's coverage had not only provided information but had served as a channel for intimidation. The American public was angry and anxious after this (and similar) incidents. It was estimated that 1.8 million Americans had changed their travel reservations to foreign countries as a result of their perception of terrorist activity abroad. Some might argue that the media-made perception was accurate. However, if one would have asked these Americans how many American civilians were killed in international terrorist incidents, it is likely that their figures would have been substantially higher than 33 (1983), 13 (1984), 23 (1985) and 19 (1986). Their refusal to go abroad meant a financial loss for the tourist industries of several countries in the Mediterranean and in Europe in general. Estimates of loss of business ranged from $100 million for Greece to $500 million for Egypt and $800 million for Italy.

The Egyptian, Greek or Italian people in their national tourist industries will never be able to decide how many minutes of coverage ABC, CBS and NBC should give to an incident like TWA Flight 847. They were indirect victims of terrorism and media portrayal of staged events. The American public was also indirectly victimized in the sense that one successful anti-American terrorist attack encourages new ones. . . .

Terrorists—Users of, or Used by, the Media?

"News" is, Jeremy Tunstall has suggested, "an Anglo-American market-based concept." Editors defend their news selection sometimes by saying that they give the public what it wants—implying that they are fulfilling a market demand. What they fail to say is that they not only provide information, but also channel intimidation to the public which, in turn, increases the demand for information as a way of reducing uncertainty. A vicious circle is set in motion into which terrorists inject again and again their electrifying newsworthy attacks. The competition between networks for scoops is fed by terrorist atrocities and terrorist communications in the videotapes they send to stations and the interviews they grant.

Terrorists use the media and the media use terrorism. At the time of the Tehran embassy incident this was particularly evident when the Canadian Broadcasting Corporation filmed a mob demonstration. As soon as the cameras were on, the demonstrators began shouting "Death to Carter," raised their fists, looked angry and burned American flags. After two minutes, the cameramen signalled the end of the "take." Then the same scene was done once more for the French-speaking Canadians, with the crowd shouting "Mort à Carter."

> *"There is . . . hope that the media themselves will one day recognize that using staged violent events from terrorists is not worth the higher ratings."*

In the debate between the people in the media and the people in government, there is much concern expressed about the media being "used" by terrorists and their sympathizers. However, the terrorists themselves also feel "used" by the media which pick up their action, but offer no guarantee of transmitting their message. Only in cases where the terrorists also control media directly can they fully control the way their violent communication is handled. Colonel Qaddafi of Libya has staged live executions for Libya's state television in 1984; other executions were shown in regular new programs from tape. Will the blood and the ink flow on forever? The fact that scores of journalists and editors have been threatened and killed by terrorists is an indication that the "friendship" between media and terrorists is not without hazards. There is, perhaps, some hope that the media themselves will one day recognize that using staged violent events from terrorists is not worth the higher ratings. If government control of news coverage on terrorism is undesirable, public control unreachable, self-regulation by the media is perhaps the only realistic option.

Towards a New Code of Ethics

The question then becomes: what should a realistic Code of Ethics look like in order to minimize the impact of violence performed with the aim of being picked up and magnified by the media? The general aim of such a code should be, as has been well expressed in a United Nations Educational, Scientific and Cultural Organization (UNESCO) document by the British veteran journalist Clement Jones: "To protect those to whom communication is made, the mass of the populace, from any irresponsible, anti-social or propaganda use of the media."

The problem, when it comes to terrorism, however, is this: if the media are to refuse playing the role of a megaphone to terrorist violence—how are they to distinguish between genuine violence which would have taken place anyway, and histrionic violence for audience manipulation? Some "genuine" violence becomes quasi-"terroristic" if broadcast, even when the perpetrator's intention was not to have a wider impact than a local one.

Let us assume that this distinction can be drawn. What next should the media do with an act of violence which is clearly media-oriented? Black out that event and keep it out of the news? It is worth recalling what happened in the case of Herostratus, the Greek, who put the Artemis temple on fire the night Alexander the Great was born. The reason we know why Herostratus did what he did in 356 B.C. was his personal confession, made under torture, that he wanted to immortalize his name. The people of Ephesus thereupon decided to counteract his intent by prohibiting the mentioning of his name. Yet one man called Theopompus leaked it and so we know. The first news blackout attempt in recorded history failed. I am afraid that there will always be a Theopompus somewhere. In open societies where media compete with each other, blackouts are difficult to bring about. In 1976 the Secretary for Northern Ireland, Roy Mason, proposed a "black out" for all reports on violence in Northern Ireland, and even went so far as to say that if the government had control over the BBC the Irish Republican Army (IRA) would be beaten. However,

> *"There are still people in the media who justify the coverage of terrorist events with a reference to the 'people's right to know.'"*

the link between publicity and some forms of political violence is not that close. In addition, a blackout of news might create rumors which can be worse than the most overheated coverage. Nevertheless, I believe that some forms of restraint in coverage are feasible. Between a blackout and saturation coverage there is room for a reasonable compromise.

Not Sending the Message

I know there are still people in the media who justify the coverage of terrorist events with a reference to the "people's right to know." This is a weak defense of the freedom of the press. If terrorist news obliterates, as in the TWA case, for more than two weeks two-thirds of all other news, nobody complains about the "people's right to know" these news items and thousands of other significant events of a day which go unreported.

However, the basic role in a Code of Ethics should be that if terrorists kill and threaten to kill non-combatants in order to create bad news, which gives them access to the mass media, the media should deny them such access. They can do it.

> *"If the purpose of terrorists is to send a message, we in the media should consider not sending it."*

After all: "News is what the newspeople say it is," Ford Rowan of the American Public Broadcasting System once said. Steve Rosenfeld, of the *Washington Post*, wrote "if the purpose of terrorists is to send a message, we in the media should consider not sending it." However, this is easier said than done. Sometimes publicity is demanded under the threat of killing hostages. The denial of access following small-scale terrorist violence might result in terrorists, producing mass slaughters which simply cannot be ignored. However, this is true for perhaps 2 percent of all terrorist groups. The others simply do not have the means for escalation. The violence output they produce already stretches their resources to the maximum.

Above, I noted that terrorists are not satisfied with the media coverage they obtain. The quantity of coverage may be sufficient, but they cannot control quality—except in the case of state terrorists. The quantity is able to confer them status, but not legitimacy. The media note the violence, but are hardly interested in the long communiqués that go with it, explaining the reason why. The consequences of this dilemma have been well put by Michael J. Kelly and Thomas H. Mitchell:

> The terrorist is in something of a trap. The media will help him attract the attention of an audience but it will not let him transmit his message. The implications of this are disturbing. By sapping terrorism of its political content, the media turn the crusader into a psychopath. This puts the terrorist in a situation where he is encouraged to continue to maim and kill without any hope of ever attaining the political support that he needs to enact the transformation he seeks. It prolongs the agony of the victimizers as well as the victims. . . . If terrorism is ultimately a battle for the hearts and minds, as the psychological

warfare approach would suggest, it seems that the press is neither a totally reliable nor a totally effective weapon. . . . The terrorist cannot discontinue his activities because his power is based on publicity, but at the same time the kind of publicity he receives deprives him of the ability to rally support for his cause. In the end it may be the media that exploit the terrorist.

Becoming Professional

The consequences of this for constructing a Code of Ethics for the media are interesting. While it is difficult to avoid terrorist use of the media without imposing censorship, it should be less difficult to curb the exploitation of the terrorists by the media. The thrust of most guidelines on media coverage of terrorism has been on how to get the terrorist story disentangled from their propaganda. Perhaps we should begin by asking how guidelines can disentangle the media interest from the public interest in a terrorist's story. In some terrorist situations, terrorists and hostages have parallel interests. Media and public interest can also parallel each other some way. Yet when informing the public becomes intimidating the public, and when this is the result not of the magnitude of the terrorist threat but of the magnitude of the coverage, there should be a line dearly drawn that should not be crossed with impunity by the decision-makers in the media.

Ultimately, the question boils down to what we wish "News" to be. Is it a social or a commercial product? If it is the latter, then indeed "Good news is bad news and bad news is good news and no news is bad news." If we decide that "News" is more than a capitalist commodity to be marketed, we must establish what is "harmful news" and perhaps also what is "pro-social news."

It is time for a new maturity that recognizes that the media do much more than just report what happens in the world. The media, and especially television, *are* the central market square in today's global society. They have power. They should therefore also carry responsibility which should find its expression in a meaningful and enforceable Code of Ethics.

> "When informing the public becomes intimidating the public, and when this is the result . . . of the magnitude of the coverage, there should be a line clearly drawn."

Sociologists define a profession by two characteristics: a Code of Ethics and rules of enforcement. The present media Codes of Ethics rarely address some of the most burning ethical problems of journalism. Only the quality papers and stations adhere to some Code of Ethics. The rules of enforcement are practically absent in most, if not all, democracies. In this sense, the people in the media are still not fully "professional."

Hate Radio Can Inspire Terrorism

by William Raspberry

About the author: *William Raspberry is a nationally syndicated columnist.*

President Clinton has spoken out against the "loud and angry voices" who use the airwaves to spread hate.

"Their bitter words can have consequences," Clinton told a Minneapolis gathering of college officials on April 24, 1995, suggesting (but stopping short of the direct accusation) that right-wing talk radio hosts may have some measure of responsibility for the violence that wracked Oklahoma City that month whether they intend such violence or not.

Naturally, these talk-show hosts have been quick to protest their innocence. They never told anyone to plant bombs or kill people, they insist—only that they should defend themselves against an overzealous government. And if some idiot listens to them and, on his own, does something awful and illegal . . . well, it's not *their* fault.

Shooting Back

That was the line G. Gordon Liddy took after the bombing of the federal building in Oklahoma City.

"Anybody who has listened to me knows that I have not advocated at any time blowing up the ATF [the federal Bureau of Alcohol, Tobacco and Firearms], the building they're in, or anything like that," he told his listeners. "What I have said is that if you are subject to a lethal attack . . . by the ATF, have a prearranged cellular call for members of the militia who can come and protect you. And if they shoot, try to kill you, shoot back. Save your life. That's obvious."

Even with his disclaimers, Liddy certainly illustrates the point the president sought to make about the "loud and angry voices in America today whose sole goal seems to be to try to keep some people as paranoid as possible and the rest of us all torn up and upset with each other."

William Raspberry, "Bomb-Throwers and Broadcasters," *Washington Post National Weekly Edition*, May 1-7, 1995; © 1995, Washington Post Writers Group. Reprinted with permission.

These voices, he said, "spread hate [and] leave the impression by their very words that violence is acceptable."

To quote Liddy: "That's obvious."

And it should be particularly obvious to G. Gordon Liddy. This is the guy who, according to testimony before the Senate Watergate Committee, heard former Nixon campaign aide Jeb Magruder remark that it would "be nice if we could get rid of" columnist Jack Anderson.

Liddy, according to the testimony, not only took the chance remark literally but also interpreted it as an order to kill Anderson—and set off to do it. He calmed down after Magruder made it clear that he intended no such action.

Observing the Obvious

Here's the point: If Liddy could misinterpret the words of a man who was sitting in the same room—a man he knew very well—and set off on an assassination mission, how can he not understand the potential danger of his remarks to strangers over the air? Can't he conceive of the possibility that his audience may include people as close to the edge today as Liddy himself was 20 years ago?

But this isn't solely about Liddy. Other flamboyant talk-show hosts—certainly including Rush Limbaugh, the most famous of them all—need to understand that their words, no matter how innocent or rhetorical or satirical they may in fact be, have the power to push certain people over the edge, into violence. I don't mean to suggest that such broadcasters should be shut up, only to remind them that it is possible to be both conservative and responsible.

And not just broadcasters. Speaking in public about forming militias to resist the government and broadcasting recipes for bombs is clearly beyond the bounds of ordinary civil discourse.

But what of Rep. Bob Dornan's repeated assertion that President Clinton is not *his* commander in chief? Or Senator Jesse Helms's warning that the president shouldn't come to a military base in his state of North Carolina without a bodyguard? (Senator Bob Dole's announcement that he would seek to un-ban the very sort of automatic weapon with which some nut had just sprayed the White House in what authorities say was an assassination attempt may not fall into the same category, but it comes close.)

> *"Talk show hosts . . . need to understand that their words . . . have the power to push certain people over the edge, into violence."*

It's not enough for these men to satisfy themselves that they meant no harm. They need to reflect on the possibility that their excessive language can lead other people over whom they have no direct control to *do* harm. They must know, as Clinton put it, that "their bitter words can have consequences."

Ask Jeb Magruder.

Publishing Do-It-Yourself Munitions Books Increases the Risk of Terrorism

by Fred Reed

About the author: *Fred Reed writes the Police Beat column for the* Washington Times.

The flap over the April 19, 1995, bombing in Oklahoma had a lot of people asking questions on the order of, "How did [primary suspect] Timothy McVeigh, if Mr. McVeigh it was, get the materials, and how did he know how to make a bomb, and why can't we control the materials?"

Lethal Titles

The questions are reasonable, but the answers, I'm afraid, aren't. An entire little industry exists to teach the lethal-minded to be lethal in reality. It's pretty amazing.

For example (there are others), in Boulder, Colorado, there is an outfit called Paladin Press. You probably haven't heard of it, but it is just a short drive from the offices of Soldier of Fortune magazine, between the two of which there has been migration of employees. Paladin sells books, to anybody at all, on how to do all manner of fascinating things. Opening the latest catalog at random, to page 68, one finds the following books:

Homemade Mortar Construction Manual; *Ragnar's Guide to Home and Recreational Use of High Explosives*; *Improvised Land Mines*; *Car Bomb Recognition Guide—How They're Made, How to Detect Them* (note that "how they are made" and "how to make them" differ in voice of verb only); *Pipe and Fire Bomb Designs*.

Would you prefer *Death by Deception—Advanced Improvised Booby Traps*, by Jo Jo Gonzales? That's page 67, catty-corner from *Improvised Explosives— How to Make Your Own*. Surely this is a comic book, you say, a joke. Nope, not hardly. "Ten simple but powerful formulas for explosives and incendiaries give you the basis to construct actual bombs, booby traps, and mines. Learn how to obtain or make all the necessary chemicals or acceptable substitutes."

How about *Guerrilla's Arsenal*, by David Harber, 168 pages? Among other socially useful tidbits, one learns "the secrets of constructing 10 different initiation delays and their pipe-bomb housings." For the technically minded, there is *Improvised Radio Detonation Techniques*, which tells the enterprising, if unsocialized, hobbyist how to use cordless telephones, pagers and cellular phones as detonators.

No Joke

These books are not fooling around. The information is real, the authors mostly competent. At the bottom of most descriptions of books one finds the caveat, "For academic study only," which may or may not provide Paladin with a degree of legal protection.

Another section of the catalog deals with lock picking, as for example *Secrets of Lockpicking*, which a blurb says is "the perfect handbook for locksmiths or anyone on the outside, itching to get in." I suspect that Paladin, if asked, would say the book is for people who have locked themselves out of their apartments. A lot of burglars can read.

Then there's *Kill Without Joy*, which covers " . . . the Hatchet Job . . . Smothering . . . Drilled to Death" and "the many terrible ways in which man has dispatched his fellow man with icy dispassion over the centuries." Five-hundred pages. Oh, joy.

Ever feel the need for a silencer for your hogleg? Then buy *How to Make a Silencer for a .45*. Or maybe *The Hayduke Silencer Book—Quick and Dirty Homemade Silencers*.

The foregoing is a small fraction of what is in the catalog, and there are plenty of other catalogs. Because I have subscribed to various legitimate police publications, I get catalogs that offer, among many other things, bottles of chemicals that ruin a car's paint, stuff to squirt into a lock to freeze it shut forever, and bugging devices.

> *"An entire little industry exists to teach the lethal-minded to be lethal in reality."*

In short, detailed technical knowledge on anything you and the nutball down the street want is out there—assassination, vandalism, serious explosives, homemade flame throwers, bugging, breaking and entering. The improvised-explosives books carefully tell you how to use things that aren't illegal and can't be traced—e.g., ammonium nitrate fertilizer—which guarantees that manufacture can't be prevented.

Can publication of this stuff be stopped?

On First Amendment grounds, I doubt it. It's all for academic study, see. Scholars and all. And the lunatic fringe, whether the Whatever Militia or the Weather Underground, has the networks and the disaffected chemistry students to do pretty sophisticated things.

I remember a flap years ago in the (excellent) British technical journal *New Scientist* over the matter of patents on nerve gas, which, like other patents, were public. Making public such information, even in a patent, sounds altogether insane, but, unless I'm insane, it happened.

Which is scary. Really, all that protects us against terrorism is that we just don't engage in it. All the FBI agents in the world can't begin to stop Joe Gaga from killing a whole lot of people—at least not if Joe is determined and willing to risk getting caught afterward. It's too easy. And Paladin is there to make it easier.

Terrorism Is Not Affected by Media Coverage

by Jeffrey D. Simon

About the author: *Currently a foreign policy consultant, Jeffrey D. Simon spent six years with the Rand Corporation as a specialist on terrorism and political violence.*

"The terrorists are manipulating the media and getting great kicks," said Daniel Schorr, former CBS and CNN News correspondent and currently senior news analyst for National Public Radio. "And it's this mindless competition [among news organizations] which causes them to do it. There really ought to be a kind of voluntary code in which they say, 'We report the news, we don't dramatize it more than it is already demanding. [And] we don't do live interviews.'" Schorr's views reflect a widely shared perception among the public, government officials, and some newspeople themselves that the media have played into the hands of terrorists by providing excess coverage of terrorist episodes and overdramatizing certain events. Yet the media have tended to be unfairly blamed for encouraging or perpetuating terrorism. This is due to several prevailing myths about terrorist-media interaction.

Terrorist PR

The first myth is that *most terrorists try to use the media to their advantage.* This implies that terrorist groups worldwide take the media into account when they plan their operations, that they time their attacks to gain maximum media exposure, and that they strive for as much publicity as possible for their various causes. This leads to the logical assumption that if media coverage of terrorism would be reduced significantly, then so, too, might be the terrorist threat.

This is a myth because only *some* terrorist groups utilize the media. The vast majority do not. For every press conference and interview session that has been conducted by a terrorist, and for every message or threat that a terrorist has issued through the media, there are hundreds of other terrorists who couldn't care less about media attention. When various car bombs were set off in crowded marketplaces in Beirut by warring Christian and Muslim factions in the 1980s, they were not done for media exposure. They were aimed instead at the civilian populations of each side as part of a campaign to demoralize them as well as to retaliate for previous attacks. The people in Beirut and in the Lebanese government would hear about these bombings regardless of the amount of coverage in the press or on television. It would be difficult for anybody living in the city not to know about the carnage. The same was true for other terrorist bombings in populated cities, including attacks by Tamil extremists in Colombo, the capital of Sri Lanka, or by Shining Path guerrillas in Lima, Peru.

State-sponsored and state-directed terrorists also tend to avoid media scrutiny or publicity for their actions. They "do not need publicity to generate recruits or sympathy," observes Patrick Clawson, a terrorism analyst. When Bulgarian agents killed a leading Bulgarian defector, Georgi Markov, in London in 1978 with a poison-tipped umbrella containing ricin, the last thing they wanted was publicity. They wanted to quietly silence the defector and leave no traces of their crime. But Markov lived long enough to tell his doctors that a stranger bumped into him on Westminster Bridge and apologized for prodding him with his umbrella. The remains of the poison pellet were found in Markov's thigh.

Media exposure for terrorists can carry risks of identification, potential capture, and possible interference or distraction with future operations. In the aftermath of the assassination of Indian Prime Minister Rajiv Gandhi, a newspaper published a photograph of the alleged assassin—a female member of a Tamil Tiger suicide squad who detonated a bomb that was tied around her waist as she bowed to greet Gandhi at a campaign rally. The photograph aided investigators in their search for those involved in the killing.

Extensive press and television coverage of a particular terrorist act can also lead to increased pressure on a government to crack down on the suspected terrorist group. While some groups, such as the anarchist Japanese Red Army and German Red Army Faction, may seek such a reaction in

> *"Only some terrorist groups utilize the media. The vast majority do not."*

the belief that it would lead to a repressive state and further their goals of "world revolution," most terrorist groups avoid that strategy. There have also been cases in which media attention to a particular terrorist incident forced the terrorist group to issue an "apology." The Irish Republican Army (IRA) and the Basque separatist group ETA claimed they were sorry for two separate bombings in Northern Ireland and Spain that killed innocent people and led to widespread antiterrorism demonstrations in both countries.

Desperate for Attention

There are, of course, terrorist groups that thrive on generating media attention. Their actions have led to the perception that all terrorism is media-related. The first group to effectively use the media was the Palestine Liberation Organization

(PLO) and its various factions. The wave of hijackings that began in 1968 were, in the words of columnist Charles Krauthammer, the origins of "media terrorism." "The terrorist acts of the PLO were not intended to demoralize the Israelis—the PLO has never really been at war with Israel—but to publicize political grievances," Krauthammer told a terrorism conference in 1983. "And the intended audience was not the immediate victims—the airline passengers—or even the Israelis, but the entire world. For such actions, coverage by the mass media becomes absolutely essential. This is where terrorists' utter dependence on the media begins."

> *"Media exposure for terrorists can carry risks of identification, potential capture, and possible interference."*

The Croatian separatists who hijacked a TWA plane in 1976 and demanded that an ideological statement be printed in several newspapers were certainly geared to using the media. Juliene Busic, who was part of the hijacking team, believes that had there been sufficient media attention to Croatian grievances before the hijacking, the terrorist act would not have taken place. "The media failed to play the role that they should [have] play[ed] prior to the hijacking," said Busic. "They are not aware that a lot of times their attention to certain issues will create conditions where people will not commit the desperate actions [they do] because they feel that they have a voice. . . . If they had done that before the hijacking, the hijacking probably wouldn't have happened." "Z"—a pseudonym for a convicted Armenian terrorist who plotted to blow up the Turkish consulate office in Philadelphia in 1982—agreed: "Armenians have generally felt that there has been a wall of silence around their cause. . . . I know definitely . . . one of the reasons [for the bomb plot was] the media issue. . . . To target a building of some sort just to cause some financial damage and to get some coverage, media coverage."

The various pro-Iranian Shiite extremists in Lebanon who seized foreign hostages throughout the 1980s were also aiming to create media attention. The terrorists were dependent on the global media to convey various messages and threats to governments about the fate of their citizens if certain demands were not met. They also knew that kidnapping Americans would get tremendous play in the U.S. press and television.

But many terrorists go about their violent business without considering media exposure. Terrorism existed before there was a mass media to cover such events, and would continue even if all reporting about terrorism ceased. The issue of terrorists manipulating the media is limited to particular terrorist groups and to particular terrorist incidents such as hijackings and hostage taking.

Images of "Crisis"

The second myth about terrorism and the media is that *the media foster images of "crisis" over terrorism.* This perception stems from the fact that it is on the television screens, in the newspapers, and on the radio that the general public experiences the dramas of a terrorist event. News bulletins, banner headlines, and round-the-clock coverage all lead to this view. But this tends to mask the influential role that presidents and their top aides play in creating a crisis atmosphere during terrorist incidents. When the public sees presidents become captive of the White House while a hostage episode is unfolding, or sees them declare a "war" on terrorism, it becomes quite easy to assume that a crisis is at hand.

While the media will seek statements from government officials and the president during terrorist episodes, they will also be the recipients of unsolicited information that the administration believes might be useful in resolving the incident. This could include issuing warnings through the press to terrorists or their state-sponsors about U.S. options if the hostages are not released, or simply acting in such a manner that the media will convey to the American people that their government is on top of the situation. All this adds to the sense of crisis over the event. "The press, especially the Washington press, is almost entirely dependent upon official sources," said *New York Times* correspondent Michael Wines. "Informed outside observers that do not have the stamp of government authenticity simply don't count. So when you get a tip from the inside that something is important, that makes it important to your editors. After that, it is up to the publisher and then the public."

Administration officials are well aware of the influential role that they can play with the media during terrorist incidents. The Carter administration was the first to see this backfire when it tried to utilize the media during the first few months of the Iran hostage crisis to rally public support around the president. By continually talking to the press about the plight of the hostages, the administration was able to keep national and international attention focused on their fate, but also on the inability of the president to free them. "How to deal with the media is a very tricky kind of thing to do," recalled Cyrus Vance, secretary of state during the Carter administration. George Shultz, secretary of state in the Reagan administration, agreed. "We live in the information age," said Shultz. "That's a fact of life. So there's no point in saying we should turn the clock back, or something like that. That's the way life is. *Achille Lauro* [a 1985 Italian cruise ship hijacking by Palestinian terrorists, in which an American was killed], we handled a lot more quickly and better

> *"Terrorism existed before there was a mass media to cover such events, and would continue even if all reporting about terrorism ceased."*

because the ship was isolated . . . and there was no media. In the case of the TWA plane [TWA Flight 847], it was wild because the terrorists in effect were putting their message out over the television." L. Paul Bremer, the chief U.S. counterterrorist official during the Reagan years, had his headaches in dealing with the press during terrorist episodes. "In the actual coverage of the incidents themselves, the press is a very tricky element," said Bremer. "I mean, I can tell you [that] in chairing our task forces during terrorist incidents, the question about how you deal with the press is—if not the first question—it is certainly the second question."

There is no doubt that in the course of competing with each other for scoops or for the most extensive coverage of a terrorist incident, the media can make life difficult for a president. "Almost every television station in every major city in the nation now has some sort of reporter in Washington," said journalist Wines. "Newspapers that ten years ago would never have thought of covering the White House on a daily basis now pack themselves into the press room. It's a different kind of atmosphere. There is a lot more pack journalism and there is a lot more competition not just to be first with the news, but to make it as spectacular and awe-inspiring as possible. It is a temptation reporters have to resist all the time."

> *"It has been the presidents themselves, particularly Carter and Reagan, who made the hostage issue a 'personal drama.'"*

But despite the media's pursuit to uncover the latest information—no matter how insignificant—about a terrorist episode, it is still those "high-level government officials" that can set the tone for how the story eventually plays out in the media. "If it [the government] wants to contain the impact of a news story, they don't have to get up every day and feed us stories to keep the story going," said Leslie Gelb, the foreign affairs columnist for the *New York Times*. "If they wanted to, if they want the handling of the crisis to take place more quietly, they have some influence on that process by how they treat us in the daily briefings and in the background."

Focusing on the "Personal"

The third myth concerning media behavior during terrorism incidents is that *the media can limit a president's options in responding to terrorism.* This myth arises, in part, from the tendency by the media to focus on the "personal" elements of a terrorist story. Many terrorist episodes are characterized by numerous television, radio, and newspaper interviews with the families and friends of hostages or other terrorism victims. There are also profiles of the hostages. Some media critics argue that this complicates a president's ability to downplay a hostage incident or to order a military rescue or retaliatory operation, since it might lead to the deaths of the hostages.

This is a myth, however, because it has been the presidents themselves, particularly Carter and Reagan, who made the hostage issue a "personal" drama for themselves and for the country. And while presidents will surely be concerned with potential public and media reaction to a counterterrorist operation, their decisions will also be based on a variety of other factors, including the probability of success of the operation and its likely geopolitical repercussions.

Another argument that is sometimes raised against the media is that they can negatively affect U.S. counterterrorist plans by disclosing information that could be helpful to terrorists or their state-sponsors. This includes the risk of tipping them off to U.S. intentions by publishing or broadcasting reports on possible responses, or discussing in detail specific plans. This argument is part of the broader debate on the responsibilities of the media in reporting national security affairs.

Knowing When to Tell

While there is no consensus as to what constitutes a report that could be deemed harmful to U.S. national security—mainly because there is no consensus on what exactly is "national security"—the media have often adhered to government requests not to publish certain information. The *New York Times* withheld publication in 1961 of a story on the secretly planned Bay of Pigs invasion at the request of President Kennedy. In the aftermath of his worst foreign policy fiasco, Kennedy reportedly joked that he wished the media *had* published the story so that he might have been forced to reverse his decision. When the Reagan administration asked the media not to disclose the fact that one of the hostages on board TWA 847 was a member of the National Security Agency—which possibly would have put his life in danger—they obliged. And although the news media reported that Delta Force had been deployed for a possible rescue operation during the TWA hijacking, they did not disclose that the special U.S. counterterrorist team had been sent to Cyprus.

The media came under heavy criticism for publicizing the deployment of Delta Force, even though that information was leaked to them by the Reagan administration for tactical reasons. "We did not say where it [Delta Force] was being deployed to," said former NBC News President Larry Grossman. "We decided to do it [announce the deployment] because it was leaked to us so that we would broadcast it. . . . I mean nobody told us that, but that was clear. But people who didn't know it was leaked yelled at the media as an example of their insensitivity and their failure to abide by security to say [that] Delta Force [had been deployed]. . . . But the government wanted the hijackers to know that we were not without our resources. And if we had said they were going to Cyprus and there were 3,200 guys and they had three tanks and twelve bazookas, that's a different kettle of fish. But we have guidelines."

> *"The amount of publicity that the media give to any particular terrorist event has little effect on its duration."*

The decision on whether to broadcast or print information that might have an impact on national security is one that is left to the editors and news executives. Their natural inclination, not surprisingly, is to keep the public informed. "I will err on the side of telling more than less," said Ed Turner, CNN's executive vice-president. "There are considerations of national security sometimes—not often—but sometimes. And we damned sure pay attention to those. But those really are not frequent major factors. A politician will say it is. And what he means is the security of this administration or this policy. But that's not truly national security. It's *their* security. And you have to be sophisticated enough to divine the difference. But we will inevitably come down on the side of more reporting, and not less, at CNN."

Not a Crucial Factor

The fourth myth about the media and terrorism is that *the media help prolong terrorist episodes by giving the terrorists continuing and widespread publicity.* This myth has arisen due to the numerous times that the public has watched on television as cameras and reporters converge on the scene of a hijacking or other hostage-type event, and then see the episode continue for days, weeks, or months.

This is a myth, though, because the amount of publicity that the media give to any particular terrorist event has little effect on its duration. Terrorists may prolong or end a terrorist episode for a variety of reasons, including their perceptions of the degree of success or failure in having their demands met, pressure from third parties or state-sponsors to take certain actions, fatigue with the hijacking or hostage ordeal, or other factors related to the politics of the country or region where the episode is taking place. The TWA 847 hijacking, for example, lasted two weeks due to the intricate politics of the Middle East. This included the jockeying for power among various Lebanese factions that wanted to exploit the hijacking crisis for their own advantage, and the difficulty in arranging a "deal" with the hijackers, Amal leader Nabih Berri, Syria, and Israel, whereby the Israelis would release hundreds of Shiite prisoners in return for freedom for the hostages. Although media coverage of the TWA hijacking turned into a circus at times, their presence was not the reason the crisis lasted seventeen days.

This was also true for the Iran hostage crisis. The militants in Iran took advantage of the media presence there to stage various demonstrations for the cameras, and the crisis became the number-one media event in the United States. But the ultimate outcome of the hostage crisis had more to do with the internal politics of Iran than with the role of the media. "I doubt, however, that even if the media had not been playing up as much as it had, that we would have gotten the hostages back earlier than we did," said Cyrus Vance. The Ayatollah Khomeini was using the hostages for his own purposes, which included maintaining a revolutionary fervor in Iran and creating a parliament, the Majlis, that would reflect his vision of an Islamic state. There was little hope of winning the release of the hostages until that stage was completed. The media attention played into the hands of the militants at times, but was not the decisive factor in prolonging the crisis.

Blaming Conservative Media Rhetoric for Terrorism Is Irresponsible

by John Corry

About the author: *John Corry is a former media critic for the* New York Times *and author of* My Times and Adventures in the News Trade.

First, there was the name-calling; then came the sullen truce. It began when Bill Clinton said he had not meant to blame Rush Limbaugh and his like-minded colleagues for the Oklahoma bombing, although obviously he had, and everyone knew it. The evening news broadcasts all led with his remarks— "They spread hate. . . . I'm sure you are now seeing the reports of some things that are regularly said over the airwaves"—and as Dan Rather pointed out, Clinton had left no doubt about "who's talking that talk." Indeed, Clinton had left no doubt at all, and much of the media immediately fell into agreement. Conservative rhetoric, it seems, had gotten out of hand; the pious bombast of a Rush or a Newt Gingrich had inspired a murderous rage in the Oklahoma bomber.

Attacking Conservatives

Some of the early comment was merely frivolous, of course—knee-jerk reactions by journalists who simply had to say something. On CNN's "Capital Gang," Juan Williams of the *Washington Post* talked about "angry white men, sort of in their natural state," and connected this with not only the bombing, but also "the right-wing triumph over the agenda here in Washington." Two days later, columnist Carl Rowan, Williams's *Washington Post* colleague, wrote that "unless Gingrich and [Bob] Dole and the Republicans say 'Am I inflaming a bunch of nuts?', you know we're going to have some more events. . . . I am absolutely certain that the harsher rhetoric of the Gingriches and the Doles . . . creates a climate of violence in America."

Vaporings like that could be ignored. Williams, after all, was appearing on television, where panelists are encouraged to blurt out provocations, especially on programs like "Capital Gang." Rowan, meanwhile, had been attacking conservatives for years, and long tenure had left him ossified. On the other hand, there was also *Post* columnist David Broder. He is widely regarded as sober and thoughtful, but on the same day Rowan was blaming "the Gingriches and the Doles," he was blaming Rush Limbaugh. It is dangerous "to inflame twisted minds with statements that suggest political opponents are enemies," he wrote. "For two years, Rush Limbaugh described this nation as 'America held hostage' to the policies of the liberal Democrats, as if the duly elected president and Congress were equivalent to the regime in Tehran. I think there will be less tolerance and fewer cheers for that kind of rhetoric."

Broder's column was a marker for where liberal commentary would now find consensus: the Gingriches, Doles, and Limbaughs had not planted the bomb, but their incendiary preachments had inspired paranoia and malignant hatred among those who did plant the bomb. By truckling to the gun lobby, condoning the apocalyptic visions of the Christian Right, and expressing contempt for government, conservative Republicans had hatched a monster. The lineage was clear. Ideas have consequences; the thought is father to the deed, and now men in camouflage gear were stockpiling weapons in sealed containers in the woods while they searched the skies for black helicopters.

Looking for Right-Wing Plots

In the aftermath of the bombing, the media went on alert. Ted Koppel even took "Nightline" to Decker, Michigan, population 100, to interview members of the Michigan Militia. The confrontation was inconclusive. Two weeks later, in a story that drew on the work of eleven reporters and a handful of stringers, the *New York Times* found that Timothy McVeigh [the main suspect in the Oklahoma bombing] had been seen at only a single militia meeting.

The media assumed the Oklahoma atrocity could not have been the work of one, two, or three madmen, but was part of a large conspiracy. There had to be a conspiracy. The carnage was so great, and the horror was felt so deeply. McVeigh could not have been acting alone, or with only a few others, any more than Lee Harvey Oswald could have been the lone assassin. If McVeigh believed, as he reportedly did, that the Army had planted a computer chip in his buttocks, he was beyond the reach of political rhetoric. He lived with only his delusions. The liberal-left, however, looks for right-wing plots. Oliver Stone may be dismissed as an eccentric, but even respectable news organizations published fantasies about the October Surprise [a theory that the 1980 Reagan cam-

> *"Bill Clinton said he had not meant to blame Rush Limbaugh . . . for the Oklahoma bombing, although obviously he had, and everyone knew it."*

paign conspired with Iranian terrorists to delay the release of American hostages until after the presidential election]. An FBI affidavit in mid-May 1995 contained nothing to indicate that the bombing had been planned or carried out by anyone other than Timothy McVeigh and Terry and James Nichols, although the press had been suggesting otherwise.

"Who are they?" *Time* asked the week after the bombing—the "they" being "Timothy McVeigh and his right-wing associates." The next week *Time* asked, "How dangerous are they?"—the "they" this time being members of "an amorphous, far-right populist movement of both armed militias and unarmed groups that harbor a deep distrust of government." *Time* also warned that "when politicians and talk-show hosts promote the idea that

"If McVeigh believed . . . that the army had planted a computer chip in his buttocks, he was beyond the reach of political rhetoric."

the Federal Government is one step away from breaking down your door, they edge toward what the historian Richard Hofstadter famously termed the paranoid style in American politics."

As an example—its only one, actually—of how the talk-show hosts were edging, *Time* quoted G. Gordon Liddy, who fatuously had told his listeners how to stop federal intruders: "So you shoot twice to the body . . . center of mass." In the hunt for right-wing rhetoricians who would, as David Broder said, "inflame twisted minds," showman Liddy was a precious find. He turned up on all the news broadcasts, and media pickings would have been slim without him. When Anthony Lewis of the *New York Times* denounced "the drumbeat of right-wing rhetoric," he naturally quoted Liddy. Otherwise, the best he could do was Gingrich, who supposedly had said that Democrats were "the enemy of normal Americans," and Limbaugh, who had used the dread word "feminazis." But as examples of inflammatory speech these weren't much, and in fact Gingrich had made the remark about Democrats not at a public gathering but in a private session before the election with lobbyists. (The *Washington Post* heard about it and ran a story. Afterwards Gingrich said he thought he had been misquoted, but that if he really had said "normal Americans" he was mistaken. He meant to say, he said, that Democrats were the enemy of "ordinary Americans.")

A Poorly Drawn Comparison

Meanwhile, the list of right-wing suspects grew. The same week Lewis's column appeared, *New York* magazine was out with a large headline, "The Un-Americans," six of whom it pictured on the cover: Phil Gramm, Oliver North, Jesse Helms, and Pat Robertson, as well as Liddy and Limbaugh. Inexplicably, Gingrich was missing, even though New York insisted that "the right-wing paranoia exposed by the Oklahoma City bombing was fueled by the outrageous rhetoric of mainstream conservative politicians." As a repository for trendy liberal opinion, *New York* is unmatched; therefore, it is well to pay attention to what it says. The Speaker of the House may not have made the cover, but the story inside, by Jacob Weisberg, insisted there was "a link between the revolutionism of 'Mark from Michigan' and the 'revolution' demanded by Newt Gingrich." It also said that discussion of the Oklahoma bombing had been conducted "on such an abstract plane, one would think that all McVeigh and Newt shared was generalized distaste for broad federal authority." On the contrary, Weisberg insisted, the "connection is far more specific and disturbing. . . . The fringe right has been a welcome guest at Newt Gingrich's party, just as the Black Panthers were at Lenny's."

Lenny, of course, was the late Leonard Bernstein, and presumably Weisberg had cited him to prove his impartiality. In the wake of the bombing, other commentators and columnists did the same; they disparaged the liberal Bernstein so that they might feel free then to trash the conservative Republicans. In fairness to Bernstein, though, it should be noted that the comparison was poorly drawn. When Bernstein threw his famous party for the Panthers—immortalized by Tom Wolfe in *Radical Chic*—he may have been pandering to thugs, but Gingrich and his allies were being accused of fomenting real violence. Weisberg's best proof for this was Gingrich's ties to the National Rifle Association (NRA).

> *"Clinton condemned 'promoters of paranoia' who speak so irresponsibly over the airwaves, but he was ignoring the fact he had done that himself."*

The Speaker, Weisberg wrote, had told the NRA that he would investigate both the raid on the Branch Davidians in Waco and the shoot-out in Idaho in which the wife and son of white separatist Randy Weaver were killed, along with a federal marshal. Weisberg also noted, as did many others, that freshman Representative Helen Chenoweth had held a hearing in Boise in which she had deplored "excessive force" by federal agents. Chenoweth, Weisberg wrote, "is probably the most extreme member of the House gun club."

Say now that the pro-gun movement includes some extremely unattractive people, and that NRA characterizations of FBI and Alcohol, Tobacco and Firearms agents as "jackbooted government thugs" are offensive. (John Dingell's characterization of the agents as "jackbooted American fascists," which he made on the floor of the House in February 1995, was offensive, too, but Dingell is an old liberal darling, and so hardly anyone noticed.) Nonetheless, the NRA, and Gingrich and Chenoweth, were surely more correct in their appraisals of Waco than liberal writers like Weisberg, or, for that matter, politicians like Bill Clinton. The Sunday after the bombing, the president displayed a stunning insensitivity toward the Waco tragedy in an interview on "60 Minutes." He claimed that what had happened in Waco did not excuse "the kind of inflammatory rhetoric that we're hearing all across this country." Then he added:

Before there was any raid, there were dead federal law-enforcement officials on the ground. And when that raid occurred, it was the people who ran their cult compound at Waco who murdered their own children.

But there were no dead federal agents on the ground before the raid. Four agents were killed, along with six Branch Davidians, when some seventy agents in commando gear stormed the compound to arrest David Koresh on a weapons charge. At the same time, Clinton's assertion that the Davidians killed their own children was grotesque. Two months after the first raid, some eighty people, including at least seventeen children, were either asphyxiated, crushed, shot, or burned to death in a misbegotten FBI attack sanctioned by Janet Reno. When the surviving Davidians were brought to trial, the jury refused to convict any of them on the government's most serious charge: conspiring to murder federal agents.

The Enemy of Choice

What could Clinton have been thinking? He had said the Waco raid did not excuse the "inflammatory rhetoric we're all hearing," but his misrepresentation of what happened at Waco could only make the rhetoric worse. The "amorphous, far-right populist movement" that *Time* described was sure to be aroused. Its deep distrust of government would be intensified. It is impossible to escape the thought now that this was unlikely to bother the White House in the least, and that there had been an element of calculation in Clinton's remarks. Politically and culturally, the amorphous right is the enemy of choice. Little is lost in provoking it. The day after his appearance on "60 Minutes," Clinton condemned the "promoters of paranoia" who speak so irresponsibly over the airwaves, but he was ignoring the fact he had done that himself.

Not Publishing the Unabomber's Manifesto Would Produce Harmful Consequences

by John Leo

About the author: *John Leo is a syndicated columnist and contributing editor for the national weekly newsmagazine* U.S. News & World Report.

Editor's Note: The Unabomber's manifesto was published by the New York Times *and the* Washington Post *on September 19, 1995. The following viewpoint, written prior to that date, remains relevant to the debate over whether to allow terrorists to have access to the media.*

The Unabomber has a 35,000-word diatribe that he wants to get published. The *New York Times* and the *Washington Post* have a journalistic principle they want to defend—nobody tells them what to print. But if they refuse to print the diatribe, the Unabomber promises to keep killing people. What on earth shall they do?

Oh, stop all the agonizing and just print it.

This is truly a no-brainer. Which is a worse outcome: People keep getting blown up by mail bombs, or the *Times* and *Post* have to run a boring op-ed article that's much longer than usual?

Real People Will Die

Let's go over that again. If the newspapers say no, real people will die. If they say yes, the only victims are the extra Canadian trees that will have to be put to sleep so the *Times* and *Post* can publish the bomber's rant.

Some would say that the publication of long and unreadable articles has been done before at both papers, even without a life at stake. Why not now? The newspapers can perform the socially useful chore of stringing the bomber along for a while, giving the Federal Bureau of Investigation (FBI) more time to draw a bead on him.

John Leo, "Unabomber's Diatribe Is His Least Risky Package," *Conservative Chronicle*, August 16, 1995. Reprinted by permission of the author.

Besides, both newspapers ran substantial sections from the Unabomber's screed the first week in August 1995. If it is OK to run 3,000 words, why is it dangerous and ethically wrong, as some commentators say, to run the whole thing? Virtually the whole journalistic establishment seems to be opposed to publishing the full text, though nobody complained about excerpts. Doesn't this mean that the real objection is based on the length of the text, not on principle?

We are told that giving in to the bomber will compromise the press and glorify a man who has killed three people and wounded 23 others. "Cover the news, yes; publish at gunpoint, no," wrote *Boston Globe* columnist David Nyhan. He wonders: "How many other weak-minded individuals will thrill to the attention this outlaw hogs, and try to replicate his outrages?"

Yes, that's a concern, but this case is unfolding much like a kidnapping: "Meet my demands or the victim will die." Under these conditions, the rational act is usually to meet the demands, avoid the murder, and try to capture the criminal after the threat of death has passed.

A lot of people seem to think that giving all that space to the bomber will set a precedent. Won't all kidnappers, bombers and hijackers demand their seven pages too? Well, no. Literary terrorists aren't very common. Killers who tap out 35,000-word manifestos and force them on leading newspapers are even rarer.

Boring Babble

Most publicity-prone offenders just want to babble on television. Or they demand the right to surrender on camera to Peter Profile of Channel 64 *Eyewitness News*. Most of the time they seem to get their way, and the republic doesn't fall. Even David Koresh got his 58 minutes on CNN.

In fact, the *Times* and the *Post* both caved in once before without setting a worrisome precedent. Both published messages by Croat hijackers in 1976. The hijacking ended peacefully and nobody mimicked the Croats' tactic for two decades.

All of this could soon be academic. By printing large gobs of the text, the *Times* and *Post* have shown the nation how the bomber argues and writes. This obviously increases his chances of being identified. A prose style isn't exactly like a fingerprint, but it is usually quite distinctive.

> *"Publicity-prone offenders just want to babble on television. . . . Most of the time they seem to get their way, and the republic doesn't fall."*

The bomber knows a lot about the history of science and may have hung around various universities for years. He has written a letter to *Scientific American*. How many technology-hating campus intellectuals write with such clarity, contempt for both liberals and conservatives, a fondness for breaking out into CAPITAL LETTERS, and a mix of high-falutin' and low-falutin' phrases? By putting this crucial identifying data on the table, the *Times* and the *Post* have performed a service. Now all they have to do is print the rest of it. They can manage this by convincing themselves that the full text is news-worthy, just like the excerpts.

The good part is that the tedious fullness of the Unabomber's argument virtu-ally guarantees that nobody will read it. A 35,000-word text is seven pages in a full-sized newspaper. Some magazine readers tolerate long articles, but the glaze starts to harden around the eyeballs of the average newspaper reader at about 1,500 words. At 3,500 words, readers' heads will begin falling into the soup all over New York and Washington. Each newspaper may have to find an insomniac just to copyread the text.

The *Times* has characterized the Unabomber's manuscript as "closely rea-soned" which means—in plain English—both "boring beyond belief," and "we're probably going to print it." And they should. If they refuse and another person dies, the victim's family and community will start shouting that the *Times* has blood on its hands. Outraged editors who now say you can't give in to extor-tion will begin switching sides and bemoaning a needless death. People will won-der why the *Times* let someone die because of pride and fear of precedent.

And the people who wonder will be right.

Chapter 4

Do Antiterrorism Measures Threaten Civil Liberties?

Antiterrorism Measures: An Overview

by Mary H. Cooper

About the author: *Mary H. Cooper is a staff writer for* C.Q. Researcher, *published by Congressional Quarterly, Inc.*

Until February 1993, Americans were secure in the knowledge that, at least at home, they were safe from international terrorists. Then Islamic fundamentalists sent a shocking wake-up call—the bombing of the World Trade Center in New York. In April 1995, Americans were shaken again when a powerful blast destroyed the federal building in Oklahoma City. But that attack—the worst case of domestic terrorism in U.S. history—apparently was perpetrated by American citizens. In response to the escalating terrorism against the U.S., the Clinton administration and the Republican-dominated Congress have presented several anti-terrorism proposals. But some observers question whether they will work, whether they are constitutional and if future terrorists will up the ante, using even more deadly techniques.

The Threat of Terrorism in America

The bombing of the Alfred P. Murrah Federal Building in Oklahoma City on April 19 is still largely a mystery. But one thing is certain: As an act of terrorism, it was the epitome of success, and not just because of the high death toll.

"The intended purpose of terrorism is to create alarm," says Brian M. Jenkins, an authority on terrorism at Kroll Associates, an international security firm based in Los Angeles. "The goal is to attract publicity to the terrorists and their causes."

As the nation now knows, the prime suspect in the bombing, Timothy McVeigh, reportedly acted in retaliation for the ill-fated federal raid on the Branch Davidian complex near Waco, Texas, exactly two years earlier [April 19, 1993]. McVeigh, a decorated veteran of the Persian Gulf War, is said to have felt that law enforcement officers trampled cult members' rights in the operation, which left more than eighty people dead, including twenty-four children.

Excerpted from Mary H. Coooper, "Combating Terrorism," *CQ Researcher*, July 21, 1995. Reprinted by permission.

The Oklahoma City attack was especially shocking to the American public because it invaded the nation's heartland and claimed so many victims. But it wasn't the first time in recent years that terrorists have targeted U.S. citizens and property. Since 1987, terrorist attacks, mainly by Middle Eastern groups, have left more than 400 Americans dead.

Until recently, however, the attacks had occurred overseas. That precedent was broken February 26, 1993, when a massive car bomb exploded under the World Trade Center in Manhattan, killing six people and injuring more than 1,000. Four Islamic militants have been convicted of the crime, and the alleged mastermind awaits trial. Ramzi Ahmed Yousef, who police say is behind terrorist acts around the globe, was arrested in February 1995 in Pakistan and extradited to New York, where he is being held pending trial. Yousef, a Kuwaiti, had been granted political asylum in the United States in 1992. . . .

Americans' horror at the arrival of terrorist violence in their streets is only matched by their worries about its impact on their way of life. Ever since the World Trade Center bombing, security measures have been tightened at public places around the country. Once expected only at airplane boarding areas, metal detectors now block free access to many public buildings. Since the Oklahoma City bombing, these annoyances can only be expected to increase.

Indeed, the familiar front entrance to the White House already has receded from public view with the closing of a segment of Pennsylvania Avenue to vehicular traffic. Travelers using Los Angeles International Airport over the 1995 Fourth of July weekend faced heightened security checks and flight delays because of a bomb threat by the Unabomber. This mysterious criminal has killed three people and injured twenty-three in numerous bombings since May 1978.

> *"Americans' horror at the arrival of terrorist violence in their streets is only matched by their worries about its impact on their way of life."*

Current anti-terrorist proposals seek to balance the conflicting goals of security and freedom. Several of the recommendations were sent to Congress by President Clinton in the wake of the World Trade Center attack and then strengthened and placed on the legislative fast track after Oklahoma City. Bills passed by the Senate and House would:

- expand the government's authority to conduct telephone wiretaps of suspected terrorists;
- allow the military to help investigate crimes involving biological or chemical weapons;
- bar Americans from contributing to international terrorist organizations; and
- make it easier for the government to deny entry to the U.S. to members of terrorist groups as well as deport suspected terrorists.

Congressional leaders generally support the anti-terrorist legislation. "It's a good bill; it's a bipartisan bill; it's a responsive bill," said Judiciary Committee

Chairman Henry J. Hyde, R-Ill., who drafted the House version.

Some terrorism experts concur. "A recurring theme in all the bills is the notion that we have never had a federal anti-terrorism statute," says Stacy Burdett, assistant director of government and national affairs at the Anti-Defamation League of B'nai B'rith, a Jewish organization that monitors civil rights and hate groups. "Suspected terrorists can get picked up [under current laws] on charges of conspiracy or visa and passport fraud. Even if, technically, you can still put someone who bombs buildings in jail, federal involvement in such a case should not have to depend upon a series of coincidences like that."

The bills' critics reject that argument and predict that the legislation, if passed, will run aground on constitutional challenges. "The Oklahoma City and World Trade Center bombings were very bad incidents, but current law already makes them illegal," says David Cole, a professor and constitutional expert at Georgetown University's Law Center in Washington, D.C. "They can be investigated under current law and prosecuted under current law."

> *"Critics . . . predict that the [antiterrorism] legislation . . . will run aground on constitutional challenges."*

Of more concern, in the view of Cole and many civil liberties advocates, are what they consider to be the bills' constitutional flaws. "There are two very serious constitutional infirmities in the legislation," Cole says. "One is imposing guilt by association on individuals for their support of non-violent activities of disfavored groups. The second is the provision that permits the government to rely on secret evidence to deport immigrants accused of being associated with terrorist activities."

As Congress continues to debate anti-terrorism legislation, experts fear that we have not seen the last of highly destructive terrorist attacks. The World Trade Center bombing indicated that terrorists may be more willing to strike with growing ruthlessness against "soft" targets such as busy streets, public buildings and transportation systems.

Before he was arrested and extradited to the United States, Ramzi Ahmed Yousef was implicated in a series of attacks that spanned the globe from New York to the Philippines to Pakistan, where he was ultimately arrested. "What this case reveals is the existence of a kind of global terrorist Internet, with different people in different parts of the world plugged into it," says Jenkins. "We now understand that there is a galaxy of dedicated Middle Eastern terrorists targeting the United States. This terrorism is quite exportable, and the notion that terrorist attacks would be confined to the Middle East or in adjacent Europe is no longer the case.". . .

Americans' Concerns over Safety and Civil Liberties

Immediately after the Oklahoma City bombing, even as they watched rescue workers bringing out victims, Americans called for tough anti-terrorist measures to protect the country from further atrocities. In a poll taken the day after the bombing, a majority of respondents supported many of the provisions of anti-terrorist legislation currently before Congress. Seventy-six percent supported restrictions on visits by people from countries with known ties to terrorism, while 63 percent supported increased surveillance of foreigners in the United States.

When it came to restricting their own freedoms, however, Americans were less enthusiastic. While an overwhelming 89 percent of respondents expected a similar attack in the near future, 58 percent said they would not support increased government surveillance of American citizens. Hence the challenge of new congressional proposals: to provide greater protection from terrorist attack without infringing on the broad civil liberties Americans claim as their birthright.

Indeed, no sooner were hearings launched to consider the proposed anti-terrorist measures than objections were raised about their impact on civil rights. Proposals to involve the military in cases involving biological and chemical weapons and to expand wiretap authority are among the more controversial elements of legislation proposed in the wake of Oklahoma City.

In an unusual departure from the partisan nature of most political debates, criticism of anti-terrorism proposals unites conservative Republicans and liberal Democrats who worry that federal agents may use their expanded powers to investigate and prosecute suspected terrorists to overstep their constitutional boundaries.

"We were pledged to protect and defend the Constitution," Representative Patricia Schroeder, D-Colo., said at a June 12, 1995, hearing on the House bill. "And I think we want to defend it rather than amend it with the bill."

Expressing his concern that law enforcement agencies might use their newly expanded powers to go after people who hold unpopular views, even in the absence of evidence that they are involved with terrorism, Representative Steven H. Schiff, R-N.M., said: "We don't want to rush so rapidly into this that we neglect the civil liberties protections that are also an important part of society."

> *"Hence the challenge . . . : to provide greater protection from terrorist attack without infringing on the broad civil liberties Americans claim as their birthright."*

A proposal that would expand the government's ability to wiretap telephone conversations of suspected terrorists was an early focus of the debate. "That is exactly the sort of thing that people point to as an apparent violation of established constitutional principles," says Steve Gardner, research director of the Coalition for Human Dignity, in Portland, Oregon, which monitors hate groups in the United States. Expanding the government's ability to eavesdrop, he says, "plays into the preset world view these folks on the radical right have, that the federal government is out to get them."

The Civil Rights of Immigrants

Some critics say the measure contains unacceptable violations of foreigners' civil rights as well. One violation, they say, would result from a proposed change in current law to allow the government to present only a summary of the evidence collected against foreigners suspected of terrorist acts. The change is intended to protect informants from retaliation, but critics say it denies suspects their rights. "Everyone in the United States is entitled to due process, whether a citizen or an alien, whether here lawfully or unlawfully," says Georgetown's Cole, who has represented eight Palestinians in a deportation case in litigation since 1987.

"Imagine the O.J. Simpson case," says Cole, "with the government coming in and saying, 'Mr. Simpson, we have evidence that you murdered your wife, but we can't show it to you. We'll summarize it for you instead. It says you murdered your wife.' You could have all the lawyers in the world, and you still would not be able to defend yourself."

Another controversial provision would prohibit charitable donations to international groups deemed terrorist by the president or secretary of state. Such a ban, civil libertarians say, clearly violates the constitutional right to freedom of association. But supporters say the measure is needed because the United States has become a major source of funding, through fundraising campaigns for hospitals and other charitable purposes, of some of the very organizations that attack U.S. interests.

> *"Some critics say the measure contains unacceptable violations of foreigners' civil rights as well."*

"Some people would say the president could use the law to designate some unpopular group as a terrorist organization," says Burdett of the Anti-Defamation League. "No one wants to see the law abused like that, but there could be a check against such an abuse. This is still the freest country in the world. It's a free society, which is why all of a sudden we are realizing that people may be raising money here to use for violent means."

Likewise, Burdett defends the proposal to give the government authority to bar members of terrorist groups from the United States. "I don't think that denying entry to leaders and influentials of terrorist groups is an infringement on civil liberties," she says. "It's a privilege to come to this country.". . .

"The American public obviously has a tremendous stake in being protected from terrorism. Representative David E. Skaggs, D-Colo., said at the June 12 hearing. "It also has a high stake in seeing that the government doesn't cut constitutional corners in providing that protection. We do not need to trade constitutionally protected rights, including the rights to privacy, free assembly [and] free speech for enhanced protection from terrorists. If that were to happen, then indeed terrorism would have achieved a real victory."

Antiterrorism Measures Threaten Civil Liberties

by Doug Bandow

About the author: *Doug Bandow is a senior fellow at the Cato Institute, a libertarian think tank in Washington, D.C.*

The reactions inside and outside of Washington to the April 19, 1995, Oklahoma City bombing were sadly predictable. Around the country was anger, desire for understanding, and hope for healing. In the halls of the White House and Congress was shock, followed by a race for political advantage and demand for more power. In short, everyone did what came most naturally—citizens worried about their country while politicians worried about their influence.

Washington's Reaction to Terrorism

This reaction was evident in attempts to brand critics of government as contributing to a "climate of hate" in which violence might occur. Needless to say, it is in the interest of presidents, legislators, and bureaucrats alike to discourage criticism. And many were quick to use the tragedy in Oklahoma City in an attempt to place themselves beyond reproach.

Second, politicians of both parties began posturing with proposals for new "counterterrorism" legislation. These bills would vest the federal government with vast new powers to wiretap, investigate, deport, use the military, and rely on secret evidence. If people don't already have reason to fear government, they certainly will if these measures become law.

Before Congress acts precipitously, legislators should answer four questions. Is terrorism so serious a threat that it requires an immediate, draconian response? Has government policy contributed to violence, like the bombing of the Alfred P. Murrah Federal Building in Oklahoma City? Do federal agencies require more power to combat terrorism? Does the law enforcement interest outweigh the rights and liberties of citizens that would be sacrificed?

Doug Bandow, "Terrorism in America: Let's Not Overreact." This article appeared in the August 1995 issue and is reprinted with permission from *The World & I*, a publication of The Washington Times Corporation, copyright © 1995.

A Serious Threat?

Is terrorism so serious a threat that it requires an immediate, draconian response? The Oklahoma City bombing was a hideous act, but, thankfully, it represents the exception rather than the rule. There were no terrorist incidents in 1994, either actual or prevented. Of eleven incidents in 1993, nine were committed by animal rights activists in one night. Over the past eleven years there has been only one incident of international origin, the February 1993 World Trade Center bombing. The State Department reports that international terrorist attacks are at their lowest level in nearly a quarter century.

Of course, even one attack is too many. But the current level of terrorist activity provides no cause for Congress to act without due deliberation. Legislators need to recognize that law enforcement agencies today often abuse their power, thereby stoking violent passions. In any case, the police already possess expansive authority to combat terrorism; Congress should honestly assess whether increasing these powers would do anything to combat real crime. Finally, legislators need to remember that it is a free society that they are attempting to protect. Marginal gains in a campaign against minimal threats are not worth the sacrifice of fundamental liberties.

Beware Government Abuse of Power

Has government policy contributed to violence, like the bombing of the Alfred P. Murrah Federal Building in Oklahoma City? Nothing can justify terrorism. Nevertheless, public officials must recognize that distrust of government is not limited to fringe groups. A 1995 Gallup poll found that an astounding 52 percent of people believed "the federal government has become so large and powerful that it poses a threat to the rights and freedoms of ordinary citizens." Four out of ten thought the danger was "immediate."

There is much to fear. Government misbehavior in Waco, Texas, against the Branch Davidians [April 1993] and in Ruby Ridge, Idaho, against Randy Weaver and his family [August 1992] was well-publicized and deadly. Yet rather than holding law enforcement officials accountable, the Clinton administration promoted one Federal Bureau of Investigation (FBI) agent, reprimanded for his role in both affairs, to deputy director. These cases, along with numerous brutal and erroneous Drug Enforcement Agency (DEA), Bureau of Alcohol, Tobacco, and Firearms (ATF), and local police raids, suggest that government power itself is a serious problem.

> *"Marginal gains in a campaign against minimal threats are not worth the sacrifice of fundamental liberties."*

Placing even greater authority in agencies that have abused their trust would only exacerbate peoples' fears of Washington. Therefore, legislators should first concentrate on reforming the present system. Unnecessary powers need to be terminated; abuses need to be curbed; accountability needs to be reestablished. Only then, when people's liberties would be less at risk, should Congress consider expanding the authority of law enforcement.

Do Federal Agencies Require More Power to Combat Terrorism?

Although Oklahoma City has become the justification for the antiterrorism bills, the alleged perpetrators of that bombing were quickly apprehended. So, too, were the bombers of the World Trade Center. Moreover, since 1989, law enforcement officials have prevented nearly as many terrorist attacks as have been committed, twenty-three compared to thirty-one. There is no evidence that federal agencies need more power to respond to terrorist threats.

Federal law already bars financial support for foreign terrorist groups. Proposals to expand this prohibition, to give the president unreviewable authority to designate groups as terrorist, and to investigate people where no evidence of a legal violation exists are unjustified. Similarly, terrorist acts, like the Oklahoma City bombing, are already against the law. There is no need to expand the definition to include literally every crime—"any unlawful destruction of property"—for example, which may be best handled by local authorities (such as animal rights activists).

The Government Has Enough Authority

The federal government already has wiretap authority for such crimes as arson and homicide; proposals to expand that power to almost any crime (including misdemeanors, in the Clinton administration legislation) have nothing to do with combating terrorism. After all, of 7,554 requests for wiretap authority submitted by the FBI since 1978, only one has been rejected by the special seven-member court that oversees the process. The many new powers being proposed by President Clinton, Senate Majority Leader Robert Dole, and others are no more necessary to the prevention of terrorism.

Does the law enforcement interest outweigh the rights and liberties of citizens that would be sacrificed? Even if increased power might marginally improve government's ability to respond to terrorism, Congress must still weigh the benefits against the costs. For example, the FBI investigative guidelines were created for a reason: the agency's Counter-Intelligence Program (COINTELPRO) resulted in spying on literally millions of law-abiding Americans from the 1940s through the 1970s. Yet this orgy of surveillance did not make America more secure. Nearly 700 FBI operations yielded a grand total of four convictions.

Similarly, the wholesale federalization of crimes would make Americans less free without making them more secure. State law already covers violent crime; existing federal law reaches special offenses, such as threats against the president. Proposals to expand federal jurisdiction combined with a broadening of the much-abused Racketeer Influenced and Corrupt Organizations (RICO) statute, enhanced restrictions on money laundering, loosening of restraints on wiretapping, and use of the military to enforce domestic law would provide numerous opportunities for government to abuse citizens' rights.

Expansion of wiretaps to almost any felony would also cost the American people more in lost liberty than any security they might gain. Today, the government is empowered to seek wiretaps in cases involving arson and homicide, typical ingredients of terrorist acts. Yet federal wiretaps rarely involve these issues. In fact, wiretapping is focused on, of all things, gambling, along with racketeering and drugs.

Other assaults on individual liberty that have been tied to terrorism include proposals to restrict habeas corpus, which requires the government to justify holding a citizen, and limit encryption software, which ensures the privacy of computer communication. Neither proposal is designed to combat terrorism. After all, habeas corpus, such a jealously guarded right that the Constitution permits only Congress to suspend its application, and to do so only during "rebellion or invasion," applies to those already in government custody. And computers have played no role in any recent terrorist plot.

> *"Despite the hideous Oklahoma City bombing, America remains largely free of terrorism."*

More closely tied to international terrorism is the proposal to allow special courts to use secret evidence, withheld from the defendant, in deportation proceedings of legal residents of the United States. Yet the right of "confrontation" is a critical procedural safeguard. Once Congress embarks upon the slippery slope of allowing the government to present arguments without giving the defendant a chance to directly respond, legislators could apply this principle against citizens in any case involving a serious crime: murder, arson, and the like. Either the courts would void such laws as unconstitutional, as they have done in similar cases in the past, or American citizens could end up appearing before a tribunal akin to that of Great Britain's hated "star chamber."

Don't Subvert Posse Comitatus

The president and Senator Dole have proposed increasing the role of the military in terrorism cases—essentially, repealing the Posse Comitatus Act [a Reconstruction-era law that forbids use of the military for domestic law enforcement] whenever the attorney general desires military assistance. At the same time, both proposals would eliminate jurisdictional restrictions on such agencies as the ATF, allowing them to act however they pleased against anything termed "terrorism."

But there are very good reasons for retaining a bright line between the military and domestic law enforcement. The Defense Department should not be diverted from its most important job of defending America from international foes. Soldiers are not trained in the niceties of civil liberties; involving the Pentagon will simultaneously militarize and centralize law enforcement, poor practices in a republic. In fact, abuses have been evident in the ongoing use of the

National Guard in drug interdiction campaigns. Similarly, reducing restraints on specialized law enforcement agencies will encourage further malfeasance by bureaucracies that already exceed their rightful authority, without any concomitant improvement in domestic security.

Terrorism obviously poses a serious threat to a free society like our own. But legislators should tailor their response to meet the threat, not garner votes. Despite the hideous Oklahoma City bombing, America remains largely free of terrorism. Congress' first task, then, should be to investigate how renegade government agencies are abusing their power and creating grievances that some misguided people believe are properly addressed through violence. Only then should legislators consider expanding federal law enforcement authority, and then only if they can do so without undermining the basic freedoms that make this nation unique—and worth living in.

Stronger Antiterrorism Measures Are Not Needed

by Nat Hentoff

About the author: *Nat Hentoff is a columnist for the* Village Voice, *and the* Washington Post *and is the author of* Free Speech for Me—but Not for Thee: How the American Left and Right Relentlessly Censor Each Other.

In the wake of the horrors in Oklahoma City, in April 1995, we are in a time of great anger—and great fear. Predictably, as in other such periods in American history, there is a mounting assault from legislators and the president on our basic liberties of association, speech, and privacy.

Calls for Increased Government Power

Bill Clinton, for instance, has called for increased government power to infiltrate, monitor, and engage in surveillance of "suspect" groups and individuals. He wants more money from Congress to provide law-enforcement personnel with the latest generation of eavesdropping technology. And he wants telephone companies to ensure that the Federal Bureau of Investigation (FBI) and other police agencies are able to wiretap the new digital computer lines.

Sanford Ungar, an expert on the FBI, tells the *New York Times* that the Bureau "is capable of some dangerous things when it gets carried away."

Throughout our history, whenever a government law-enforcement agency has been given expanded power, it has been carried far, far away from the Constitution. Bill Clinton, in his slippery way, is also targeting speech. On *60 Minutes* on April 23, 1995, he warned: "We should all be careful about the kind of language we use and the kind of incendiary talk we have. We never know who's listening or what impact it might have."

But not only members of militias might be listening. Other interested eavesdroppers—under the expanded personnel and powers Clinton is giving to the FBI—will be stealthy members of the Bureau. Remember the FBI's 1983 invasion of the Committee in Solidarity with the People of El Salvador? Thousands of files were opened on Americans who had little or no association with the

Nat Hentoff, "The Schumer-Clinton Assault on the Constitution," *Village Voice*, May 9, 1995. Reprinted by permission of the author.

Committee—which, by the way, was entirely lawful. The chilling effect on free speech lasted quite a while.

A History of Threats to Liberty

One of the most dangerous aftermaths of the atrocities in Oklahoma City is the rush of support in Congress for the Omnibus Counterterrorism Act of 1995—introduce by Congressman Charles Schumer (Democrat of Brooklyn) on behalf of that distinguished civil libertarian Bill Clinton.

Before exploring this un-American bill, it's worth placing what's happening now in Congress and in the White House in historical context.

Our liberties are never secure. Only seven years after ratification of the Bill of Rights, Congress—spurred by Federalist président John Adams—passed the Alien and Sedition Acts. There was fear among the populace of French "plots" against the government, so it was essential to crush any spoken criticism of the president and Congress.

In 1918, the Sedition Act made it a crime to "encourage resistance" to the United States by criticizing, in speech or writing, the government or the Constitution (!). More than 1500 people were arrested for disloyalty, among them the socialist labor leader Eugene Debs.

The most drastic attack on the Bill of Rights took place during the "Red Scare" beginning in 1919 under the obsessive direction of attorney general A. Mitchell Palmer. The great fear then was that the Bolsheviks, from their triumphant Russian base, had planted subversives in the United States. Given the signal, these domestic Reds would take over this land and enslave its people.

On January 2, 1920, the Department of Justice orchestrated a hot pursuit of suspected members of the Communist and Communist Labor parties. Prepared by private spies and agents provocateurs, a dragnet was cast over 33 cities in 23 states, and the catch was more than 4000 alleged radicals. Four days later, another official expedition to save America scooped up 6000 more.

In its zeal, the Justice Department, supposedly empowered to seize only dangerous aliens, also picked up many American citizens and many who belonged to neither the Communist nor the Communist Labor parties. Or to any political party.

The searches of membership books, correspondence, and anything else in sight totally disregarded the Fourth Amendment. Other massive violations of the Constitution included holding prisoners incommunicado—thereby violating their right to a lawyer—and detaining prisoners for excessive periods of time without their having a chance to be heard by a judge. And, of course, the massive arrests were made without warrants.

> *"There is a mounting assault from legislators and the president on our basic liberties of association, speech, and privacy."*

As for the dangerous radicals who were rounded up, a Detroit citizens' committee noted—as reported by Robert K. Murray in *Red Scare: A Study in National Hysteria, 1919–20*—that most of the prisoners crammed into jails were just "plain, ignorant foreigners who were completely unaware of why they were being so treated."

In Newark, New Jersey, a man was hauled in because he "looked like a radical." And in Hartford, Connecticut, visitors to jailed suspects were also imprisoned. (If you visit a Communist, you must be one.)

In charge of supervising the deportation cases that were the poisonous fruit of these raids was twenty-four-year-old J. Edgar Hoover.

The 1995 Counterterrorism Act

We are now in a time of Terrorist Scare, with a corollary war on the Constitution. Congressman Charles Schumer has introduced the Omnibus Counterterrorism Act of 1995.

As an index of how infectious this need to nail terrorists at the expense of the Bill of Rights has become, a companion bill has been brought in the Senate by Joseph Biden (Democrat of Delaware) and Arlen Specter (Republican of Pennsylvania). Both senators used to pride themselves as protectors of civil liberties.

They have now lost their credibility as men of courage and independence.

> *"Whenever a government law-enforcement agency has been given expanded power, it has been carried far, far away from the Constitution."*

Schumer had little credibility to lose in this regard. An ardent supporter of punishing "hate speech" and an equally fervent defender of cruelly rigid mandated sentencing laws, his authorship of this "anti-terrorist" bill is no surprise.

A *Washington Post* editorial distills the Schumer bill's chilling contempt for the Constitution:

" . . . aliens accused of supporting terrorist organizations (*the president makes this unreviewable determination*) could be tried in special courts and deported on the basis of evidence they were not allowed to see. Does this sound like American justice? . . (Emphasis added.)

"The administration's bill is unnecessary to curb actual terrorism and is instead directed against those who might have supported, for example, the *political* activities of the Irish Republican Army, the African National Congress, or any other such group." (Emphasis added.)

"The real horror of the administration's bill," continues the *Washington Post*, "is apparent in its procedural aspects. The accused is arrested, detained without a right to bail, and brought for a hearing before one of five U.S. District Court judges chosen for this responsibility by Chief Justice William H. Rehnquist." (Another distinguished civil libertarian.)

At that hearing, if the government shows that introducing certain classified information would pose a threat to the national security—by revealing the name of an informant, for example—the evidence can be used *but kept secret from the alien and his attorney. Not even a summary of the evidence need be provided.*

"*A ruling in the government's favor cannot be appealed, but a ruling against the government can, and that appeal can be heard outside the presence of the alien or his attorney.*"

The Law's Effect on Immigrants' Rights

"Thus, a person who is not a citizen can be accused by a neighbor of having supported the *political* activities of the Palestine Liberation Organization (PLO), brought before a special court, denied the right to know the evidence against him, and deported without even learning the identity of his accuser." (Emphasis added.)

You would not know it from Schumer or Clinton, but the Supreme Court has consistently ruled—as in *Kwong Hai Chew v. Colding* (1953)—that "Once an alien lawfully enters and resides in this country, he becomes invested with the rights guaranteed by the Constitution to all people within our borders. Such rights include those protected by the First Amendment [such as freedom of association] and the Fifth Amendment [you can't be deprived of liberty without due process of law].

"None of these provisions," the Supreme Court has declared, "acknowledges any distinctions between citizens and resident aliens. They extend their inalienable privileges to *all persons* and guard against any encroachments on those rights by federal or state authority." (Emphasis added.)

David Cole, a law professor at Georgetown University in Washington, D.C., and a lawyer for the Center for Constitutional Rights in New York City, has led the fight against Schumer's guilt-by-association bill in his *Legal Times* columns and on the air.

During a National Public Radio interview, Cole pointed out that "the Clinton administration's bill does not stop at immigrants. It makes it a crime for any U.S. citizen to support the lawful activities of any organization that is designated as terrorist by the president in an unreviewable designation, so the restrictions on associative freedoms are extended to citizens as well as immigrants. . . ." (Citizens, under this law, are subject to up to ten years imprisonment or a fine of up to $50,000.)

> "*We are now in a time of Terrorist Scare, with a corollary war on the Constitution.*"

"Under this law," Cole continued, "non-citizens can be deported for sending humanitarian aid to a hospital if that hospital is run by an organization which has engaged in any unlawful act. For instance, anyone who supported the activities of Nelson Mandela would have been deportable because the [African National Congress] ANC had engaged in unlawful [violent] political acts."

With this law as a weapon, imagine how President Ronald Reagan would have reacted against anyone who had supported the *nonviolent* work of the African National Congress.

Civil Liberties in Times of "Crisis"

In 1988, Justice William Brennan spoke at the Hebrew University Law School in Jerusalem. The intifada [the Palestinian uprising against Israeli rule]—and the reaction to it by Israeli troops—was close by. Brennan's subject—using the United States as an example—was how to develop a body of civil liberties law in "Times of Security Crises."

"After each security crisis ended," Brennan said, "the United States has remorsefully realized that the abrogation of civil liberties had been unnecessary. But it has been proven unable to prevent itself from repeating the error when the next crisis came along."

There's always a Schumer.

Antiterrorism Measures Threaten Immigrants' Civil Liberties

by David Cole

About the author: *David Cole is a professor of law at Georgetown University Law Center in Washington, D.C., and an attorney with the Center for Constitutional Rights in New York City.*

Editor's note: In October 1995, Omar Abdel-Rahman and his followers were convicted of the 1993 conspiracy to commit terrorist bombings in New York City, and in January 1996 Abdel-Rahman was sentenced to life in prison.

On July 3, 1993, the *Washington Post* ran a cartoon, "Let's Play Where's Abu?" Above a mass of faces was the caption: "In the crowd of immigrants below, the terrorist Abu Ben Fotwa El Fadwa El Fatweh is carrying a huge bomb strapped to his waist. Can you find Abu? If you can do it in under 20 seconds, score 100. Under 40 seconds, score 50. Any longer and you are dead meat!"

Nativist Paranoia

The cartoon neatly captures the nativist paranoia sparked by recent events: Several of the men arrested for the February 1993 World Trade Center bombing and the alleged plot to attack buildings and tunnels in New York City happened to be Arab immigrants. The public response has been to focus not on criminal activity but on Arabs and immigrants as a class.

New York magazine followed the World Trade Center bombing with a cover story, "The Arab Connection." A.S. Ross, a *San Francisco Examiner* columnist, warned that "for every violence-prone Muslim arrested, there are many more within the ranks of America's fastest-growing religion, ready and willing to do the bidding of a blind Egyptian cleric, or any number of Mideast-based terrorist organizations." He proposed making "membership in a violence-prone, or criminal-led organization" grounds for deportation.

David Cole, "The Scapegoats," *Nation*, July 26-August 2, 1993. Reprinted with permission from the *Nation* magazine; © The Nation Company, L.P.

Even the liberal establishment has jumped on the bandwagon. National Public Radio's Daniel Schorr suggested that the Immigration and Naturalization Service (I.N.S.) should focus not on "Mexicans and Haitians and Chinese" but on "terrorists in the Middle East." And the *New York Times* led off its Week in Review section on the Fourth of July, 1993, by maintaining that "easy immigration and due process" have rendered us vulnerable to domestic terrorists.

Sacrificing Immigrants' Civil Rights

It is often said that civil liberties are the first casualty of war, whether the war is on communism, crime or terrorism. But it would be more accurate to say that *immigrants'* civil liberties are the first casualty. Seventy-four years ago [in 1919] the United States was shaken by a series of politically motivated bombings, including an explosion in Attorney General A. Mitchell Palmer's living room. No evidence implicated immigrants in the attacks, but then as now anti-immigrant feeling was high. The Justice Department responded by launching nationally coordinated raids in thirty-three cities, arresting more than 6,000 immigrants suspected for their connections to radical causes. The suspects were beaten, thrown into "bull pens," tortured into signing confessions and threatened with deportation. Only 556 of the 6,000 were ultimately deported, most on charges of merely associating with communist groups.

The Palmer Raids are a stain on our history, but we seem not to have learned their lesson. Even before the 1993 arrests in New York, Senator Alfonse D'Amato introduced a bill that would expel all members of Hamas [a Palestinian liberation group], whether or not they have ever engaged in or supported an illegal act. And Representative Olympia Snowe has circulated a bill that would bar entry to all members of "terrorist organizations" and to anyone who "advocates terrorist activity." Both laws would resurrect the principle of guilt by association that led to the Palmer Raids.

On the enforcement side, the Justice Department has arrested Sheik Omar Abdel Rahman, raising questions that it too is engaging in guilt by association. Until the arrest, the department contended that it did not have sufficient evidence to implicate the sheik in either the World Trade bombing or the subsequent plot. But when political pressure mounted, the Justice Department moved to detain him under immigration law. Legally, it may do so only if he poses a risk of flight or danger to the community. It seems unlikely that a blind cleric fighting to stay in the United States poses a risk of flight. And if the government had insufficient evidence to charge him in the recent events, what evidence does it have that he is a danger to the community?

> *"It would be more accurate to say that* **immigrants' civil liberties are the first casualty** *[of a war on terrorism]."*

On another front, the I.N.S. has spent six years and probably millions of dollars attempting to deport two permanent residents of Palestinian descent who, it admits, have neither engaged in nor supported terrorist acts. They are charged with supporting an organization that has allegedly sponsored terrorism, but the I.N.S. concedes that the organization also engages in a wide range of wholly legal activity.

America must be ready to respond to acts of terror, carried out or planned, with the full force of law. For those who kill or injure civilians for political ends, long prison terms and deportation are appropriate; punishing immigrants who merely associate with unpopular groups is not. Instead of asking "Where's Abu?" we should be asking, Where are America's principles?

Cracking Down on Terrorism Is the Wrong Response

by Richard Stratton

About the author: *Richard Stratton is editor and publisher of* Prison Life, *a bimonthly magazine.*

Week one of the revolution. America is shocked; America is horrified. America is terrorized.

Terrorism Comes to America

This does not happen in the good old U. S. of A. is the common refrain. We are used to hearing of acts of political terrorism abroad. Pan Am flight 103 [destroyed by a bomb over Lockerbie, Scotland, in December 1988]; the hijacking of the Achille Lauro cruise ship [in October 1985]; the murder of athletes at the 1972 Olympic Games in Munich, Germany, to mention but a few. And we are accustomed to seeing the black-masked faces of the perpetrators. We expect them to be revealed as Palestinians, Arabs, bearded and mustachioed foreign types. Even the bombing of the World Trade Center in New York City [in February 1993] was understandable in these terms: it was foreigners, aliens, guys with names like Ibrahim and Mohammad.

And New York, well, that's not really America anyway. We can deal with terrorism when the threat comes from outside our hallowed nation. All we have to do is round up all the bad guys, those foreigners who hate America, and kill them. We need not bother ourselves with such questions as why others hate America so much as to kill innocent civilians and children. For, make no mistake, most foreign acts of terrorism are directed at America.

Now I look at the photo on the cover of our local paper. Under the headline, *Suspects Nabbed*, I see a face not unlike the faces of the cops and agents who surround the suspect. An American face, if there is such a thing. This guy has a *crew cut*, that most American of haircuts. His skin is as white as Bill Clinton's.

Richard Stratton, "Upping the Stakes," *Prison Life*, July-August 1995. Reprinted with permission.

He even looks a bit like our president with the prominent nose, the long face. He's clean-shaven, maybe blue-eyed. But his mouth is set in a tight-lipped gash, his countenance pinched and focused with stony resolve as cries of "baby killer" and "bastard" are hurled at him from an enraged crowd of his fellow Americans. He makes no attempt to hide his face.

Think of the shock and horror—*the terror*—many straight citizens felt upon realizing that this guy is an American. Americans did this. White-skinned, red-blooded Americans planted a bomb in front of a federal building in Oklahoma City [in April 1995], blew to bits a full third of the huge federal edifice, killing scores of other Americans, mostly federal workers, yet among them many—and here is the word again—*innocent* children. I read from a published list of the confirmed dead: Baylee Almon, age one; Anthony C. Cooper II, aged two; and a woman, aged fifty-one, with my last name—perhaps a relative. I am saddened, deeply grieved by the loss of lives that should never have been sacrificed in the violent political arena.

The Reasons for the Bombing

Who does not lament the death of innocent children? All children are innocent. We love them for their goodness, their innocence, and our hearts are rent with grief when we see a tiny body carried in a rescue worker's arms. I have two little boys, one just turned three, the other not quite one. I know how I would feel if my kids had been blown to smithereens in this catastrophic act of homegrown political terrorism. I would want to kill the terrorists. I would want to beat them to death with my bare hands.

My oldest boy could see that his dad had been obsessed with the news. When he saw a photo of the devastated Alfred P. Murrah Federal Building, he asked me what had happened to it. I told him someone blew it up. Then he asked me a simple question, an innocent question most three-year-olds ask thirty times a day: Why?

This is the only question that matters, particularly now that the damage has been done. *Why?* Why would white-skinned crew-cut Americans attack their own government? I spoke to a retired federal agent within hours of the bombing, before anyone knew who the bombers might be, and he called it: "BATF [Bureau of Alcohol,

> *"White-skinned, red-blooded Americans planted a bomb in front of a federal building in Oklahoma City."*

Tobacco, and Firearms] is in that building," he said. "It is two years to the day since the Waco debacle on [April 19, 1993]. It could have been anyone. Everyone hates the federal government."

Everyone hates the federal government. Certainly many of the people I know, not all of them radicals or ex-cons, hate the government. Or if they don't hate the government itself, they hate what the government does with the money it extorts from taxpayers.

I said aloud, when I heard of a probable connection to the militia movement, "Thank God it came from the right. Now maybe they will pay attention."

The President's Response

Then I saw our president on *60 Minutes*. He did the most irresponsible thing the president of a supposedly civilized nation could do: He called for more blood, more killing; expressed more anger and hatred. He said, in so many words, that the government will find the people responsible, hunt them down and kill them. The country has a federal death penalty and the president vows he'll use it, as though more death will heal our critically wounded nation.

The president said the government would do exactly what I thought I would want to do had my kids been among the victims. I'm sure the crowd that greeted suspect Timothy McVeigh outside the courthouse would gladly have torn him to pieces. But the purpose of civilization, and the role of government, is to protect us from our most primitive impulses. We expect more from the head of a government

> "[President Clinton] called for more blood, more killing; expressed more anger and hatred."

that prides itself on its moral leadership. We know in our hearts that killing is never the enlightened response.

When Mike Wallace mentioned Waco, Clinton got pissed off. His face contorted into a harsh glare reminiscent of the look on Tim McVeigh's face. Waco was no excuse, no reason. The Branch Davidians killed themselves, proclaimed the president. It was their fault. It is all right when the government kills because the government is always right.

Good God, I thought, *doesn't this man realize what he's doing?* He is *upping the stakes*. He is threatening with violence men who thrive on violence, men whose *modus operandi* is violence and destruction. He is challenging dedicated killers and urging them to kill more Americans. By declaring yet another over-reaching war, war on domestic hate groups by responding with threats of violence, Clinton is playing into the hands of right-wing militants and precipitating a crackdown that will cause more Americans to hate their government. The government's response is to never ask why people abhor its tactics, never to admit it might be wrong to kill and wage war on whoever disagrees with its mandates.

Americans Loathe Government Violence

President Clinton would call me a "promoter of paranoia." Yet are we paranoid when our own government declares bloody war upon vast segments of the people? And not just criminals or drug dealers, but many innocent people whose rights are trampled and whose homes are invaded, whose property is seized, whose lives are destroyed by the actions of federal agents.

Newt Gingrich flew into a rage when a reporter suggested that the people accused of blowing up the federal building in Oklahoma espouse views similar to those mouthed by him and his boys. *Get the government off our backs.* Of course he got pissed. Newt doesn't believe his own rhetoric. That's just politics. Lies. Like Clinton. Clinton lies. He tells us it's okay when the federal government kills American citizens and innocent children. He tells us the children of the Branch Davidians burned themselves to death because their parents weren't ready to knuckle under to the government.

Waco is not an excuse, not a reason. There is no excuse for killing innocent children and civilians. It is an example of why Americans have come to fear and loathe the government. I can give you many better examples of why Americans hate the federal government. How about when the Federal Bureau of Investigation firebombed MOVE homes in Philadelphia [in May 1985], killing innocent children. Let's talk about how many innocent children the American government has killed. How about the thousands of Panamanians slaughtered by American troops sent in [1989–90] to arrest Central Intelligence Agency asset Manuel Noriega for dealing drugs? Who can forget the image of a naked Vietnamese girl running from her village as it was razed and burned by American government troops? And I can tell you true stories of innocent, law-abiding Americans who have had their homes invaded by federal agents, been shot, been arrested, had their property destroyed or seized, all with the OK of some lying informant looking to curry favor with his federal masters. No one is ever called to task for these acts of governmental terrorism.

Thank God this guy McVeigh is not an ex-con. Can you imagine the outcry? But no, he's an ex-soldier. What does that tell you?

The Government Is a Bunch of Terrorists

Let's get it right. No one condones the killing of innocent children or innocent people for that matter. It is not right when terrorists do it any more than it is right when agents of the federal government do it. Take it further. When agents acting on behalf of the government kill children or citizens—whether innocent or not—it is government-sponsored terrorism. The death penalty is government-sanctioned murder. By vowing to hunt down and kill the perpetrators of the Oklahoma City bombing, Clinton degrades himself and lowers the government he heads to the level of the terrorists. It is gangland logic. You kill one of ours, we'll kill one of yours. The situation perpetuates itself and escalates. Where we needed dignity, restraint and measured leadership, we got bloodthirsty anger and more hate.

Clinton and others in Washington are clamoring for increased federal powers to counteract domestic terrorism. As if this weren't the problem to begin with. Wake up, Bill, Newt and the rest of you fools down there in the Capitol. There are thousands, perhaps hundreds of thousands, maybe millions of good Americans out here who hate our government. And for good reason. They are a bunch of terrorists.

Antiterrorism Measures Do Not Threaten Civil Liberties

by James Q. Wilson

About the author: *James Q. Wilson is the Collins professor of management at the University of California, Los Angeles, and is the author of* The Moral Sense.

The central question raised by the Oklahoma City bombing is whether a free society can prevent terrorist acts. A good deal of loose talk will be heard about the subject . . .—some of it urging the Federal Bureau of Investigation (FBI) to "do whatever is necessary," and some of it cautioning the government to "protect the Constitution." We have been through this before, and we ought to remember what we learned in order that we not, again, lose our bearings.

Terrorist groups, like any other criminal conspiracies, are best attacked by infiltration. This means either planting an undercover agent in their midst or recruiting one of their members as an informant. This is the job of the FBI.

If we are being terrorized by a foreign conspiracy, the bureau has rather wide discretion; if the conspiracy is a homemade one, it has a bit less. Until 1976 the bureau had a free hand in these matters. Today, however, it operates under two sets of written guidelines, one secret and one public, but both approved by the Attorney General. The secret guidelines specify the circumstances under which the FBI is allowed to penetrate groups thought to be agents of a foreign power. The public rules, which govern intelligence gathering aimed at domestic groups, are more restrictive. Yet the FBI can actively gather intelligence even on a group with political or religious sponsorship provided the bureau has credible reasons to believe the group may engage in violence. The threat of violence need not be imminent; it need only be plausible.

These guidelines were put in place in the aftermath of the COINTELPRO (Counter-Intelligence Program) scandal of the early 1970s, when it was revealed that the bureau was not only infiltrating but disrupting and harassing ex-

James Q. Wilson, "The Case for Greater Vigilance," *Time*, Essay column, May 1, 1995. Reprinted by permission of the author.

tremist organizations. First issued in 1976 by Attorney General Edward Levi and later modified by Attorney General William French Smith, the rules give the bureau authority to investigate by means that include, if necessary, "recruitment or placement of informants in groups, 'mail covers,' or electronic surveillance," provided the "facts and circumstances reasonably indicate" that a group "is engaged in an enterprise for furthering political or social goals wholly or in part through activities that involve force or violence."

There is disagreement as to whether these rules are too restrictive. In my view there is no major problem with the guidelines, but there may be one with their interpretation. FBI agents have learned to be politically risk averse. Every senior official remembers the 1976 Church Committee criticism of the FBI for burglarizing the offices of "domestic subversive targets" and bugging the rooms of Dr. Martin Luther King Jr. Some critics even suggested that the bureau end its intelligence gathering.

In the end, the Church Committee did not go that far, but the bureau conspicuously pulled in its horns. It learned another lesson a few years later [in 1980] when it captured on video members of Congress taking bribes from undercover agents posing as Arab businessmen. The public was outraged at the Congressmen, and juries ultimately convicted seven of them, but Congress was upset with the FBI and launched an inquiry into the bureau's Abscam investigation. And then in 1988 the FBI got into trouble for investigating CISPES (the Committee in Solidarity with the People of El Salvador), a group it believed was supporting leftist rebels in that country contrary to the U.S. backing of the legitimate government.

The intelligence guidelines under which the FBI operated would not have barred infiltration of the group responsible for the Oklahoma bombing, assuming that anybody had heard of it in advance. But the bureau has been whipsawed so many times by contrary political pressures—"Stop terrorism!" "Protect civil liberties!"— that many of its top officials may have adopted a perfectly understandable bureaucratic reaction: "Who needs the trouble? If there is any doubt, leave it alone."

> *"In my view there is no major problem with the guidelines, but there may be one with their interpretation."*

I believe the bureau has stopped many terrorist actions, including bombings, because it has penetrated groups it thought might use violence. It cannot take public credit for this; to do so would compromise its methods and alert its targets. I don't know whether it has prevented as many as it might have if all its members had been enthusiastic instead of cautious about intelligence work aimed at sensitive political targets.

Political support for intelligence work swings like a pendulum. This quickly changing congressional environment, while understandable in its own terms, is not helpful to a law-enforcement agency. The behavior of rank-and-file government workers cannot be fine-tuned like a clock or made precisely sensitive to changing legislative moods. The members of any organization take their cues from the general posture of their superiors and clients. When the posture is threatening, the reaction is predictable: Pull back.

Let's hope that did not happen in this case and will not happen in the future. The FBI ought to be, and is, committed to defending the Constitution. It doesn't need instant experts, immediate second-guessing or quick fixes from any quarter. If Oklahoma City is a trumpet announcing a long siege, we all need, as they say in the Navy, to take an even strain.

Stronger Antiterrorism Measures Are Needed

by Eugene H. Methvin

About the author: *Eugene H. Methvin is a senior editor at* Reader's Digest.

In February 1995, a former leader of the Michigan Militia, Eric Maloney, visited the Federal Bureau of Investigation (FBI) and warned that Timothy McVeigh and the Nichols brothers had attended a "special operations session" three months earlier where they talked about blowing up buildings. Maloney told Brian Ross, an ABC News investigative correspondent, that the FBI turned a deaf ear. "I told them that if they didn't act on this, a whole lot of people are going to get killed," Maloney said. But the FBI was not interested because "there was nothing they felt they could do."

America's Destroyed Domestic Intelligence Capacity

In the shadow of the Oklahoma City bombing, the campaign to keep America safe for terrorists revived. Rescuers were still digging victims out of the rubble when liberals leaped to their pulpits to warn against reviving the FBI's "domestic spying." They thus continued a twenty-year campaign that has destroyed the nation's domestic intelligence capacity and left Americans pathetically vulnerable to atrocities like the one in Oklahoma. They have erected a false mythology about the agency's past alleged sins. Thus the *New York Times* wailed about the FBI's and Central Intelligence Agency's (CIA) "brazen violation of American freedoms" and "contempt for the Constitution."

FBI Director Louis Freeh did mount a modest defense of law enforcement's preventive role. In testimony before the Senate Judiciary Committee he complained: "For two decades the FBI has been at an extreme disadvantage with regard to domestic groups which advocate violence. We have no intelligence or background information on them until their violent talk becomes deadly action. . . . I do not support broad and undefined intelligence collection efforts—but . . . the first rule of self-defense is to know the enemy who intends to destroy you. Intelligence . . . helps to protect the American people. It should not be considered a 'dirty word.'"

But a dirty word it is today. In the 1970s the nation allowed its domestic anti-terrorism apparatus to be crippled and virtually disbanded. Leading the destruction was a coalition of conscientious civil libertarians and radical revolutionaries dedicated to destroying constitutional government in the United States.

In 1971, the American Civil Liberties Union (ACLU) announced that "dissolution of the nation's vast surveillance network" would henceforth be a top priority. It launched a "police surveillance project" headed by Yale Law Professor Frank J. Donner, identified in sworn testimony by three witnesses as a steadfast member of the Communist Party in its worst Stalinist days. The National Lawyers Guild, whose president declared its goal was "to keep the road clear of legal roadblocks" for revolutionaries, filed lawsuits wholesale against local police intelligence units, crippling them or destroying them altogether. Old Left lawyer William Kunstler once boasted, "I stay in this profession only because I want to be a double agent, to destroy the whole ———— system."

The *Washington Post* and *New York Times* aided these crusades in both news and editorial columns. On December 22, 1974, the *Times* launched a major "exposé" of the sins of American intelligence agencies on the domestic front. This "scoop" was based on an internal study of the CIA ordered by Director William Colby, in which subordinates were instructed to review the agency's twenty-five-year history and report every activity that

> *"In the 1970s the nation allowed its domestic anti-terrorism apparatus to be crippled and virtually disbanded."*

might have violated a domestic law. Colby naïvely handed the study over to *Times* reporter Seymour Hersh, and the newspaper treated it as a major scandal.

The U.S. Senate, meanwhile, created a select committee under the chairmanship of Frank Church, the Senate's most intense left-wing ideologue. In March 1976, after more than a year of bombardment by Church and others on Capitol Hill, Attorney General Edward Levi, trying to position the weak Ford Administration for the approaching election, imposed "guidelines" on the FBI prohibiting any investigation without "specific articulable facts giving reason to believe that an individual or a group is or may be engaged in" criminal activities.

This requirement for a "criminal predicate" totally abandoned law enforcement's preventive and peacekeeping functions. In the words of one jurist, "It means every terrorist gets one free blast." Five days before Levi issued his guidelines, the FBI's intelligence division had 4,868 domestic security investigations going. Six months later there were 626. By August 1982 Congress found the number had dwindled to 38.

A Wave of Terrorism

The high cost of this destruction of domestic intelligence was demonstrated exactly a year after Attorney General Levi issued his guidelines. In Washington, D.C., a black Muslim guru named Hamaas Abdul Khaalis and eleven followers, wielding guns and machetes, seized hostages in the B'nai B'rith headquarters, the Muslim Mosque and Cultural Center, and the District of Columbia Building—Washington's "city hall." The Hanafi Muslims (as the cult called itself) killed one person and crippled another for life in their violent takeover. The siege lasted two days before the 137 hostages were released. The Metropolitan Police Department revealed that it had withdrawn an informant from the Hanafi Muslims and destroyed their file, in response to pressure from the ACLU and other police baiters. The Senate Subcommittee on Criminal Laws and Procedures in a 1978 report asserted that if the police had had an informer in the Hanafi ranks, "the chances are 100 to 1 that they would have had intelligence enabling them to take preventive action."

> *"This requirement for a 'criminal predicate' totally abandoned law enforcement's preventive and peacekeeping functions."*

It was a different story in Maryland in 1978. State Police Sergeant John Cook infiltrated the Ku Klux Klan and fed the FBI reports on its violent plottings. The FBI opened a preliminary investigation under the Levi guidelines, but closed it when nothing had happened in ninety days, as the guidelines mandated. Fortunately, the Maryland State Police did not follow the FBI's lead. They kept Sergeant Cook in place, and he worked his way into a ten-man Klan "death squad." Eventually the Klan attempted a series of bombings, including one at the home of a black congressman, Parren Mitchell. The night of their planned attacks Sergeant Cook had the pleasure of arresting.

Terror Network U.S.A.

On October 20, 1981, in Nyack, New York, a dozen Black Liberation Army (BLA) and Weather Underground terrorists killed a Brink's guard, wounded two others, and made away with $1.6 million. At a police barricade five miles away they killed two cops and wounded a third. Four of the robbers were captured and the cash recovered, but eight or more escaped.

Tracing auto tags noted by witnesses, the FBI found several terrorist lairs. Seized documents showed the group was moving to a more vicious level of urban guerrilla warfare. A list profiled two dozen corporate executives and contained biographies, photos, and daily schedules of top New York and New Jersey police officials. Plots for bombings and ambush murders were evident in hand-drawn floor plans and photos of police stations and barracks. The terrorists also had a file on former president Richard Nixon's residences. The evidence revealed a nationwide alliance of radical groups: the BLA, the Weather Underground, the separatist Republic of New Afrika, the Puerto Rican FALN. They even had links to radical feminists who ran a remote California commune where Sara Jane Moore engaged in target practice before her 1975 attempt to kill President Gerald Ford, and where the Symbionese Liberation Army kidnappers prepared their abduction of Patty Hearst and their murder of Oakland's black school superintendent, Marcus Foster. The allies had pulled off at least eighteen "armed expropriations" with more than a million dollars in loot, and had freed notorious terrorists from prison. Incredibly, this Terror Network U.S.A. had operated for over five years without either police or FBI intelligence catching a hint of the connections. In those five years the FBI's informants in political-terrorist groups had been cut from 1,100 to fewer than 50, and its domestic security investigations from 20,868 to only 10 groups and 47 individuals.

The FBI had followed the Weather Underground from its beginning, when it spun off from the Students for a Democratic Society in 1969. The investigation continued after the 1976 Levi guidelines because the Weather terrorists had committed numerous bombings—including at the U.S. Capitol, the Pentagon, and some eighteen other targets—prior to March 1974. But in October 1981 an FBI official admitted that "federal intelligence reports" were dropped in 1979 because the Weather gang "has not been active since it claimed responsibility for the 1977 bombing of a federal building in Seattle."

So unless a terrorist network announces itself periodically with press releases claiming credit for its bombings, the FBI will not chase it? That was the practice if not the disclosed rule—and continues almost so today. And the G-Men had good reasons to drop their pursuit of the Weather terrorists. Incredibly, the Carter Justice Department had more than two dozen lawyers and a grand jury investigating 132 FBI agents for alleged civil-rights violations of relatives and friends of fugitive terrorists, while none pursued the terrorists themselves.

The CISPES Scandal

In 1988, the anti-intelligence combine battered the FBI again just to keep the watchdogs intimidated. The Center for Constitutional Rights (CCR), founded in 1966 by Kunstler and three other Old Left lawyers, used the Freedom of Information Act to obtain from the FBI some 1,200 pages of files on the Committee in Solidarity with the People of El Salvador (CISPES).

The *New York Times* and *Washington Post* promptly disseminated the FBI's outrages. "FBI agents took photographs of marchers and recorded their automobile license numbers," *Times* reporter Philip Shenon panted. "Agents were also authorized to begin surveillance of students at Florida State University." And the *Post*'s Howard Kurtz seemed slack-jawed that "FBI agents investigated nuns, union members, and college students; checked up on church forums and Knights of Columbus dinners; photographed protestors at peaceful rallies; and distributed what they deemed offending articles from student newspapers and *People* magazine." Neither the *Post* nor the *Times* gave its readers any hint of what

> *"Incredibly, this Terror Network U.S.A. had operated for over five years without either police or FBI intelligence catching a hint of the connections."*

153

had triggered the FBI probe—evidence indicating that CISPES militants might be sheltering the terrorists who had perpetrated the November 7, 1983, bombing of the U.S. Capitol.

Leon Trotsky, founder of the Red Army and one of the twentieth century's chief theoreticians and proponents of terrorism, proclaimed, "No terrorist group can function without a screen of sympathizers." CISPES clearly fit the definition of a terrorist screen. In May 1980 Fidel Castro ordered the various Marxist paramilitary factions warring against the Salvadoran government to form a unified command as the condition for greater East Bloc support. The new umbrella organizations—the military Farabundo Martí National Liberation Front (FMLN) and its political/diplomatic arm, the Revolutionary Democratic Front (FDR)—launched a program to build support inside the United States. Shortly thereafter, conventions of leftists were held in Los Angeles and Washington, and CISPES was born.

> *"So unless a terrorist network announces itself periodically with press releases claiming credit for its bombings, the FBI will not chase it?"*

In 1983 the FBI learned that individuals in contact with the FDR/FMLN planned to establish clandestine cells in the United States to commit murders, sabotage, and bank robberies in support of the Salvadoran guerrillas. On March 30 headquarters authorized eleven field offices to investigate CISPES locally. Within a month, a bomb had exploded at the National War College in Washington, D.C. Numerous bombings followed—including the one at the U.S. Capitol—and anonymous "communiqués" proclaimed solidarity with the Salvadoran insurgents.

CISPES members were the prime suspects until late March 1984. Then the FBI learned that some of the Nyack fugitives and their allies were responsible. However, as a result of its investigation, the FBI was able to head off the disruptive demonstrations CISPES was planning at the GOP (Republican) convention in Dallas. The FBI continued its investigation until June 1985.

The entire CISPES investigation involved the equivalent of five fulltime agents working over two years, and cost little more than $800,000. After the *Times* and *Post* horripilations the Justice Department's Office of Professional Responsibility and the FBI's inspection division spent almost that much investigating the CISPES investigation in order to mollify the Kunstlerites, the *Times*, the *Post*, and their congressional claque. The Senate Intelligence Committee faulted the Bureau for investigating the whole CISPES organization instead of a few specific suspects. But how was the FBI to know who the suspects were, or how extensive their network was, without looking? And who can say what mischief or mayhem the surveillance prevented—thereby coincidentally protecting the constitutional rights of the large majority of CISPES members to protest peacefully?

Penetrating the Screen of Sympathizers

The current criminal-conduct-only guidelines ignore the well-documented sociology of terrorist movements. Such movements contain only a few who will build and plant bombs, or lay and execute ambushes. But many will give the actors support: medical help, money, hiding places, intelligence, and such. These support networks must be built in advance of the onslaught. Building them requires *words* to attract and recruit sympathizers. This is the stage at which prevention is possible; and if prevention fails, swift apprehension can limit the damage.

Thus in June 1970 an FBI informant within the Black Panther Party warned of a planned ambush on Detroit police, and named the designated attackers. On the appointed day

> *"Penetrating the terrorist's screen of sympathizers requires intelligence ... that can be obtained only with ... clandestine operations."*

two snipers riddled a police cruiser with armor-piercing bullets. Miraculously the two officers were only wounded. The killers were intercepted when they returned to their residence, and sent away for long prison terms. Three other named Panthers scouting another section of Detroit for a diversionary target were caught with illegal weapons and sent to jail as well.

Penetrating the terrorist's screen of sympathizers requires intelligence of a surgical precision that can be obtained only with the full arsenal of clandestine operations: informant networks, electronic surveillance, covert action.

Immigration Laws Should Be Reformed to Prevent Terrorism

by Allan C. Brownfeld

About the author: *Allan C. Brownfeld is a syndicated columnist and a contributing editor of the* St. Croix Review.

Editor's note: Omar Abdel-Rahman was convicted of masterminding a 1993 conspiracy to commit terrorist bombings in New York City, and in January 1996 he was sentenced to life in prison.

The arrest in July 1993 of a group of Muslim fundamentalists for allegedly plotting to bomb the United Nations and other targets in New York City and to assassinate such public figures as U.N. Secretary Boutros Boutros-Ghali and Senator Alfonse D'Amato (R-N.Y.) highlights the need for a dramatic overhaul of our immigration laws.

How Sheik Abdel-Rahman Came to the U.S.

Federal investigators say that new suspects, like those arrested in March 1993 in the World Trade Center bombing, are followers of Egyptian Sheik Omar Abdel-Rahman.

Why is Abdel-Rahman still in the United States? The extremist Egyptian cleric has been cited for inspiring terrorism in both Egypt and the U.S. Yet, the Clinton administration has neither arrested him nor deported him. A look at his immigration status tells us a great deal about what is wrong with both our laws and our law enforcement.

Sheik Abdel-Rahman is the man who issued the "fatwa" or Islamic sanction for the 1981 assassination of Egypt's President Anwar Sadat, according to the Egyptian authorities. Why was he permitted into the U.S. in the first place? Why is he still here now, using the U.S. as a base for fund-raising and to foment terrorism?

When he entered the U.S. in 1990 on a tourist visa, he was on the official

Allan C. Brownfeld, "Immigration Laws Need a Complete Overhaul to Protect Americans from Terrorism," *St. Croix Review*, April 1994. Reprinted with permission.

U.S. terrorist list. The State Department, in the wake of the World Trade Center bombing, finally acknowledged that U.S. government officials twice acted in error in giving Abdel-Rahman permission to enter and remain in the U.S. In first granting him a visa in 1990, the U.S. Embassy in Khartoum, Sudan, overlooked the fact that he had already been placed on a "lookout list" because of his role in fomenting violence in Egypt. Even after that visa was revoked, the Immigration and Naturalization Service (INS) office in Newark, New Jersey, mistakenly granted him permanent residence status in April 1991. The government rescinded that status in February 1992. Sheik Rahman, however, did not leave the U.S. after that decision. Instead, he applied for political asylum—a process which, with its various levels of appeal, can take years.

Because of our confused legal system, which apparently puts the safety of American citizens last, a known advocate of terror and violence who was admitted to the U.S. illegally remains at large. While in the U.S. Rahman has raised funds to promote terror in Egypt. In taped broadcasts sent back to Cairo from Jersey City, Rahman urged fundamentalists to kill Western tourists in Egypt in order to weaken the government and replace it with fundamentalist Muslims. Egyptian government spokesmen say that they believe the followers of Rahman are responsible for at least two assassinations in Egypt, that of parliament speaker Rifaat Mahgoub in 1990, and secularist author Farag Foda in 1992. They also accuse him of sanctioning the recent wave of Islamic militant attacks against foreign tourists in Egypt.

The Immigration System Is Abused

The Egyptian sheik is, unfortunately, not an isolated case. Illegal aliens, many from the Third World, have been enabled to enter the U.S. and bring their violent politics to our shores. Murders in front of the Central Intelligence Agency in suburban Virginia in January 1993 were tied to Mir Aimal Kansi, a Pakistani who was in the country illegally and has since vanished from sight.

Our system of granting political asylum cannot be permitted to continue. Nationwide, more than 250,000 foreigners are waiting in line to see one of only 150 asylum officers. Some have been waiting for years. Many of those who apply for asylum are abusing the system, U.S. officials say, using it as a way to improve their economic status rather than to flee repression.

"Our system of granting political asylum cannot be permitted to continue."

In the case of Sheik Abdel-Rahman, an immigration judge ordered him deported, but he could remain in the U.S. for years under the current system as his lawyers press his appeal through the courts. Former New York governor Mario Cuomo said that the U.S. should apprehend the sheik and "keep him secure while you are processing him. Everyone agrees our asylum laws are silly." The INS can detain aliens who arrive without proper credentials or who seek asylum for persecution in their native countries. But the INS rarely does so, contending that it doesn't have enough employees to stand guard—or enough beds to put them up.

Between 1988 and 1990, 489,000 aliens scheduled to be deported could have been locked up—but the INS has only 6,000 beds, forcing it to release more and more suspects. In 1982, the General Accounting Office reports, 24 percent of those apprehended were detained; in 1990 only 9 percent. Deportable aliens comprise 26 percent of all inmates in federal prisons. In California alone, up to 15 percent of the inmates in state prisons are thought to be deportable aliens.

> *"The chances of stopping any terrorist from entering the U.S. right now are nearly zero."*

The ability of Third World immigrants to easily enter the U.S. without documentation has been described as a "crisis" which has reached "out of control" levels. Benedict Ferro, INS district director in Rome, sent a cable to Washington stating, "Alien smuggling" through New York's John F. Kennedy Airport "has passed the crisis level, with hundreds of aliens with bogus documents or no documents at all arriving and claiming asylum." Another INS official notes that "a disturbingly high percentage of people arriving by air with no legitimate documentation are people from areas where there is a terrorist environment. The chances of stopping any terrorist from entering the U.S. right now are nearly zero."

A Worthwhile Reform

New York's Governor Cuomo, a Democrat, and Senator D'Amato, a Republican, state that asylum-seekers should no longer be allowed to roam free for years as immigration judges wait to hear their cases. In the House of Representatives, Republican congressmen have unveiled legislation to "slam the door on terrorists" and update the State Department's widely criticized Automated Visa Lookout System (AVLOS). The new "Visa Denial to Terrorists" bill was introduced by Representatives Benjamin Gilman, Olympia Snowe, and Bill McCollum. It would require the immediate automation of all overseas visa operations. "We can no longer afford a system that allows people like Sheik Rahman, who has allegedly been linked to a terrorist organization like the Islamic Group, to slip into the country by mistake." The proposed bill would also pin responsibility for issuing visas on the Foreign Service officials who issued them.

This is a worthwhile reform, but much more is needed. Those who apply for asylum must not be permitted into the American society until their claims have been properly investigated and an affirmative determination made. The process of endless appeals must be stopped. And in the case of Sheik Abdel-Rahman, who is wanted for terrorist acts in his own country, no basis of asylum exists at all.

Our government's primary responsibility is to the safety and security of the American people. Placing us at risk from foreign terrorists who are permitted to take advantage of our free and open society is highly irresponsible, if not suicidal. And the U.S. Constitution, as one Justice pointed out, is not a suicide pact.

Bibliography

Books

James A. Aho — *This Thing of Darkness: A Sociology of the Enemy*. Seattle: University of Washington Press, 1994.

Terry Anderson — *Den of Lions*. London: Hodder and Stoughton, 1993.

Michael Barkun — *Religion and the Racist Right: The Origins of the Christian Identity Movement*. Chapel Hill: University of North Carolina Press, 1994.

Yossef Bodansky — *Target America: Terrorism in the U.S. Today*. New York: Shapolsky Publishers, 1993.

Stephen Bowman — *When the Eagle Screams: America's Vulnerability to Terrorism*. Secaucus, NJ: Carol Publishing Group, 1994.

Steven A. Emerson and Cristina Del Sesto — *Terrorist: The Inside Story of the Highest-Ranking Iraqi Terrorist Ever to Defect to the West*. New York: Villard Books, 1991.

Steven Livingston — *The Terrorism Spectacle*. Boulder, CO: Westview, 1994.

Brigitte L. Nacos — *Terrorism and the Media: From the Iran Hostage Crisis to the World Trade Center Bombing*. New York: Columbia University Press, 1994.

Robert G. Picard — *Media Portrayals of Terrorism: Functions and Meaning of News Coverage*. Ames: Iowa State University Press, 1993.

Dick J. Reavis — *The Ashes of Waco: An Investigation*. New York: Simon and Schuster, 1995.

Kevin Jack Riley and Bruce Hoffman — *Domestic Terrorism: A National Assessment of State and Local Preparedness*. Santa Monica, CA: Rand Corporation, 1995.

Lyman Tower Sargent — *Extremism in America: A Reader*. New York: New York University Press, 1995.

James D. Tabor and Eugene V. Gallagher — *Why Waco? Cults and the Battle for Religious Freedom in America*. Berkeley and Los Angeles: University of California Press, 1995.

Periodicals

Nathan M. Adams — "The Terrorists Among Us," *Reader's Digest*, December 1993.

Bibliography

Jonathan Alter	"Jumping to Conclusions," *Newsweek*, May 1, 1995.
Michael Barkun	"Militias, Christian Identity, and the Radical Right," *Christian Century*, August 2–9, 1995.
David Barsamian, Chip Berlet, and Holly Sklar	"Militias and Conspiracy Theories," *Z Magazine*, September 1995.
Alan W. Bock	"Ambush at Ruby Ridge," *Reason*, October 1993.
Angelo Codevilla	"Anti-Terrorism or War?" *National Review*, July 10, 1995.
Marc Cooper	"Montana's Mother of All Militias," *Nation*, May 22, 1995.
James X. Dempsey	"Bombing the Bill of Rights," *Rights*, July–September 1995.
Diana R. Gordon	"The Politics of Anti-Terrorism," *Nation*, May 22, 1995.
Jane Hunter	"Bill of Wrongs," *In These Times*, May 1, 1995.
David S. Jackson	"On the Moderate Fringe," *Time*, June 26, 1995.
Kathleen Morris	"Profits from Paranoia," *Financial World*, April 25, 1995.
Robert Perkinson	"Oklahoma Fallout," *Z Magazine*, July/August 1995.
Christopher Phelps	"Angry, White, and Armed," *Against the Current*, July/August 1995.
Progressive	"The Far Right is Upon Us," June 1995.
Llewellyn H. Rockwell Jr.	"The Bomb," *Rothbard-Rockwell Report*, June 1995. Available from PO Box 4091, Burlingame, CA 94011.
Kirkpatrick Sale	"Unabomber's Secret Treatise: Is There a Method in His Madness?" *Nation*, September 25, 1995.
Jill Smolowe	"Sheik Omar Speaks Out," *Time*, March 15, 1993.
Mack Tanner	"Extreme Prejudice: How the Media Misrepresent the Militia Movement," *Reason*, July 1995.
Time	"Defending Islam," October 9, 1995.
Jacob Weisberg	"Playing with Fire," *New York*, May 8, 1995.
Philip Weiss	"Outcasts Digging In for the Apocalypse," *Time*, May 1, 1995.
Tim Wheeler	"Behind the Oklahoma Bombing," *Political Affairs*, June 1995.
Mortimer B. Zuckerman	"The Inside-Outside Wars," *U.S. News & World Report*, May 8, 1995.

Organizations to Contact

The editors have compiled the following list of organizations concerned with the issues debated in this book. The descriptions are derived from materials provided by the organizations. All have publications or information available for interested readers. The list was compiled on the date of publication of the present volume; names, addresses, fax numbers, and phone numbers may change. Be aware that many organizations take several weeks or longer to respond to inquiries, so allow as much time as possible.

American-Arab Anti-Discrimination Committee
4201 Connecticut Ave. NW, Suite 500
Washington, DC 20008
(202) 244-2990

This organization fights anti-Arab stereotyping in the media and lobbies elected officials on issues of interest to the American-Arab community; it organized lobbying efforts against certain provisions of the 1995 Omnibus Counterterrorism Act. It publishes a series of issue papers and a number of books and can provide bibliographies on issues such as terrorism and hate crimes.

American Civil Liberties Union (ACLU)
132 W. 43rd St.
New York, NY 10036
(212) 944-9800

The ACLU is a national organization that works to defend Americans' civil rights as guaranteed by the U.S. Constitution. It publishes memoranda on the threat to civil liberties by counterterrorism measures. It also maintains the interactive computer forum "Constitution Hall."

Anti-Defamation League (ADL)
823 United Nations Plaza
New York, NY 10017
(212) 490-2525

The ADL works to stop the defamation of Jews and to ensure fair treatment for all U.S. citizens. It advocates the adoption of antiterrorism laws and antiparamilitary training statutes by state and federal governments to fight domestic terrorism. It publishes the monthly *On the Frontline* newsletter and the periodic *Terrorism Update* report and distributes reports such as *Armed and Dangerous: Militias Take Aim at the Federal Government.*

B'nai B'rith Canada
15 Hove St.
Downsview, ON M3H 4Y8
CANADA
(416) 633-6224
fax: (416) 630-2159

Affiliated with the Anti-Defamation League, this organization works to stop the defamation of Jews and to ensure fair treatment for all Canadian citizens. It monitors violent extremist groups and advocates antiterrorism measures in Canada, and it publishes the annual *Review of Anti-Semitism in Canada*.

Cato Institute
1000 Massachusetts Ave. NW
Washington, DC 20001-5403
(202) 842-0200

The institute is a libertarian public policy research foundation dedicated to stimulating debate on foreign and domestic policy issues, including terrorism. Its *Policy Analysis* on current topics is published periodically and the *Cato Policy Review* is published every other month.

Center for Democratic Renewal
PO Box 50469
Atlanta, GA 30302-0469
(404) 221-0025

Formerly known as the National Anti-Klan Network, this nonprofit organization monitors hate group and white supremacist activity in America. It publishes the bimonthly *Monitor* newsletter and periodic special reports such as *Militias: Mainstreaming Racism and Bigotry* and *The Militia Movement: In Their Own Words and Deeds*.

Center for the Applied Study of Prejudice and Ethnoviolence
The Prejudice Institute
Stephens Hall Annex
Towson State University
Baltimore, MD 21204-7097
(410) 830-2435

The center conducts research on topics related to prejudice and violence, including prejudice and the mass media and neo-Nazi hate groups. It publishes the quarterly newsletter *Forum* as well as numerous reports.

Council on American-Islamic Relations (CAIR)
1511 K St. NW, Suite 807
Washington, DC 20005
(202) 638-6340

CAIR is a nonprofit membership organization dedicated to presenting an Islamic perspective on public policy issues and to challenging the misrepresentation of Islam and Muslims. It fights discrimination against Muslims in America and lobbies political leaders on issues related to Islam and Muslims. Its publications include the quarterly newsletter *CAIR News* as well as the periodic *Action Alert*.

Greenpeace USA
1436 U St. NW
Washington, DC 20009
(202) 319-2444

This international environmental organization consists of conservationists who believe that verbal protests against threats to the environment are inadequate—it takes action. It publishes the quarterly newsletter *Greenpeace* and periodic *Greenpeace Reports*.

The Heritage Foundation
214 Massachusetts Ave. NE
Washington, DC 20002
(202) 546-4400

The foundation is a public policy research institute dedicated to the principles of free enterprise and limited government. It publishes occasional papers on current public policy issues in its periodic *Backgrounder*, among them "The Changing Face of Middle Eastern Terrorism."

Southern Poverty Law Center/Klanwatch Project
PO Box 2087
Montgomery, AL 36102
(205) 264-0286

The center litigates civil cases to protect the rights of poor people, particularly when those rights are threatened by white supremacist groups. The affiliated Klanwatch Project and the Militia Task Force collect data on white supremacist groups and militias and promote the adoption and enforcement by states of antiparamilitary training laws. The center publishes numerous books and reports as well as the monthly *Klanwatch Intelligence Report*.

U.S. Department of State
Bureau of Public Affairs
Office of Public Communications
Washington, DC 20520
(202) 647-6575

This federal agency advises the president on the formulation and execution of foreign policy. It maintains the Counterterrorism Rewards Program to help apprehend terrorists and was instrumental in capturing and extraditing suspects in the 1993 New York World Trade Center bombing. It publishes the annual report *Patterns of Global Terrorism*.

Index